APOSTLE AND BISHOP

A Study of the Gospel, the Ministry and the Church-community

A. G. HEBERT, S.S.M.

The problem of Christian Reunion is one to which churchmen of all denominations have given close attention in recent years. Conversations between Canterbury and Rome, between Canterbury and the Eastern Orthodox Churches, and between the Church of England and the non-episcopal denominations compel the attention of the laity as well as of the clergy, and are followed not only by the religious press but much more widely. A contribution to the subject by so distinguished a liturgical scholar as the Reverend A. G. Hebert of the Society of the Sacred Mission is sure to stimulate discussion. His arguments will be warmly defended, and perhaps as warmly contested, wherever the problem of reunion is debated.

Fr. Hebert's point of departure is *The Apostolic Ministry*, a book in which he had a share, edited by the late Bishop Kirk of Oxford and published in 1946. *Apostle and Bishop* is brief, and the argument is densely concentrated. The author's approach is best described in his preface, which tells us that he is 'not thinking really in terms of "validity" and "invalidity" (of Holy Orders) but more in terms of what the Christian minister does as president in the Liturgy, as preacher of the Word, and as pastor of the Flock'. He says modestly that with each chapter 'a really adequate and scholarly treatment would demand a whole volume'. But within the compass of this book great learning is combined with very subtle and cogent reasoning.

Apostle and Bishop

APOSTLE AND BISHOP

A Study of the Gospel,
the Ministry and the Church-community

by
A. G. HEBERT, D.D.
of the Society of the Sacred Mission

THE
Seabury Press

New York

Contents

★

7

Contents

Preface

★

The starting-point of this book is the fact that I had a share in *The Apostolic Ministry*, which was edited by Bishop Kirk of Oxford and was published on December 2nd 1946; in the writing of it, I have sometimes imagined myself to be writing an extended review of that book. As I have explained in the first chapter, I am reaffirming its positive thesis and upholding the Catholic view of valid orders, but rejecting the negative inference that all non-episcopal sacraments and ministries are simply invalid. Yet that statement of the matter is not quite correct; for as I have been told by a Brother of my Community, I am striking out a partly different line, not thinking really in terms of 'validity' and 'invalidity', but more in terms of what the Christian minister does as president in the Liturgy, as preacher of the Word, and as pastor of the Flock. It was an awareness of this that caused me to write that it has been and is an Anglican fault to present Episcopacy simply as part of the Law and Constitution of the Church. The wisest review of my book on *Fundamentalism and the Church of God* (S.C.M., 1957) was one by the American Dr. Marty in the *Christian Century*, who in a delightful way interpreted for me my own thought; perhaps someone will do the same for this book.

With such a liturgical and theological approach, it is not possible for me to 'lay down the law' in the way that a book on Validity of Ministries would require. In that case, I should have had to say precisely what ought to be done with regard,

Preface

for instance, to the vexed problem of Intercommunion. I did in fact make an attempt to deal with that problem in my final chapter; but I found that a brief treatment of it was most unsatisfactory, and that only a full discussion of it would be of any use. I felt sure that such a discussion would have attracted a disproportionate amount of attention from reviewers and readers, and would have distracted their attention from the things that I really had to say in the book. For this reason I am saying nothing about it, and am leaving the discussion of it to others who are more closely in touch with the actual problem.

My duty in this book, as I see it, is to clear up such historical points as can be cleared up, and above all to try to make clear the theological points which underlie the study of the Christian Ministry. Some of these are controversial points; and here I want to reaffirm what I said on pp. 14–16 of *Fundamentalism and the Church of God*, that it is a mistake in controversy to try to refute one's opponents. In that case, if one wins the argument, one has really lost it; for those whose views have (perhaps) been successfully refuted will only be hardened in their opposition. The better way is to try to set out the principles, and to believe that the Holy Spirit is able to lead those who disagree to learn from one another—we from them, and they from us. Above all, in all that concerns Christian Unity, there has got to be agreement and concord in the Truth, the truth which the Holy Spirit teaches. We can be one only if we agree to be one.

The argument of the book proceeds thus. Chapter I is introductory. Chapters II–IV are mainly historical; I start with the gospel history, in order to show the relation of Apostolate and Episcopate to our Lord's Gospel-message. Chapter V is of central importance, for it deals with the faults of the middle ages and the protest of the Reformation; but at the end two problems are left unsolved, those of eucharistic sacrifice and of the nature of the ordained ministry. Chapter VI must therefore make a fresh start, dealing with Priesthood and Sacrifice in the Scriptures; then Chapters VII and VIII deal with the Eucharist in relation to the Accepted Sacrifice of Christ, and with the relation of the Ordained Ministry to the universal Priesthood

Preface

of All Christians. In conclusion, Chapter IX affirms that in a real sense the non-episcopal churches are true churches, and their ministries real ministries; then follows a brief discussion of possible Ways of Unity, and finally a statement of what the Office of the Bishop really is, as the only possible basis for a reunited Christendom.

The pith of the argument is that till the end of the patristic period the development of the Ministry takes a straightforward course; Episcopacy was everywhere accepted, and the fatal breach between West and East in the eleventh century involved no dispute about that, but only about Primacy. The real problem in the West arises from this, that the errors and corruptions of the Middle Ages were so serious that in the sixteenth century and after it Lutherans and Reformed and Anglicans and Roman Catholics were all compelled to labour to set right what had gone wrong; but each tradition did this in its own way, separately from the others and mostly in a state of hostility towards them, and later of uneasy toleration. It is only recently that they have started to make studies of the positive value of one another's remedies, and so to prepare for a new Reformation both of the Protestant reformation and of the Counter-reformation, such as might provide a basis of concord sufficient for a widespread recovery of visible unity. The Orthodox East is here of great value to the West, because it has not shared in its errors and its efforts to remedy them.

Quotations from the Old Testament are almost always from the *Revised Standard Version* for the Old Testament, and those from the New Testament from the *New English Bible*; for permission to quote, I have to thank Thomas Nelson and Sons and the Oxford and Cambridge University Presses, respectively. I have similarly to thank Messrs. Hodder and Stoughton for the quotations from *The Apostolic Ministry* on pp. 77–8 and 143–4, and many other references to that book; the Society for Promoting Christian Knowledge for those on pp. 68–9, 111–12, 115–16, and 129–30; Messrs. Longmans for those on pp. 85–6 and 123; the Epworth Press for those on pp. 101–2 and 134–5;

Preface

the Faith Press for one on p. 138–9; Bishop Lesslie Newbigin and the Australian Council of Churches for those on pp. 135–6 and 140–2; Messrs. Darton, Longman and Todd for the use of material on pp. 71–6; Professor Prenter of Aarhus for much material between pp. 85 and 88, and 131 and 134; Fr. Boris Bobrinskoy for the material on pp. 124–7; and Les Editions du Cerf, Paris, for that on pp. 146–8.

I have to thank several of the Brothers of my Community, and also the Rev. Fr. Benedict Green, C.R., the Rev. A. M. Allchin, and the Rev. V. de Waal, for much helpful criticism. And finally I wish to thank Messrs. Faber and Faber for once again accepting a book from me; for they were the publishers of that which I reckon as my first, *Liturgy and Society*.

GABRIEL HEBERT, S.S.M.

House of the Sacred Mission,
Kelham, Newark

CHAPTER I

The Aim of this Book

*

(i) *A controversy about Church Order*

In May and October 1961 the two Convocations of the Church of England were called upon to consider two schemes for United Churches, in Ceylon (Lanka) and in North India and Pakistan respectively, and to pronounce whether they would be prepared to recognize these proposed united Churches and be in communion with them. The two schemes were on the same general lines, but differed in detail since the uniting bodies in the two cases were not the same. Both schemes proposed an Episcopal Ministry, and both proposed a Rite of Unification for the presbyteral order of the ministry. The chief question at issue in the Convocations was whether the rite of unification was theologically sound. In it, episcopal hands were to be laid on all presbyters, both those who had already been episcopally ordained and those who had not; and it was acknowledged that no minister could be asked or allowed to deny the reality of his previous ministry, when by this rite all were constituted as Presbyters in the Church of God, within the new United Churches. The question then was, just what this rite of unification would be, in view of the different answers that would be given to the question whether it was or was not an ordination. In the eyes of many of the Anglicans, the Ministers who had not been episcopally ordained would need and would then receive for the first time a valid ordination; but in the eyes of those men themselves, it would not be an ordination but rather the extension of their Ministry to authorize them to minister to Christians to whom they had previously not been able to minister; and exactly the same would be held by all the Anglicans of what was being done for themselves in this rite, when hands were laid upon them. Did these schemes of union then involve a fatal ambiguity? Or was it right to say, as those who were responsible for the schemes had been saying, that such a seeming ambiguity was necessarily involved in the repairing of so anomalous and dreadful a thing as a schism between Christians, because on such an occasion they would be calling upon the Lord of the Church for a new creative act to initiate a healing of a schism within the Church which is his Body?

The Lambeth Conference of all the Anglican bishops in 1958 had judged the Ceylon Scheme to be sound, and had given a general approval to the Scheme for North India and Pakistan, subject to the reconsideration of certain points in it. In the debates in the two Convocations in 1961, the Upper House (of Bishops) agreed all but completely with the view that had been taken at Lambeth; but the Lower House (of Clergy) were almost equally divided, for and against, so that in almost every vote the majorities were small. York Convocation in May gave the answer No; Canterbury reached no decision in May, and in October gave the answer Yes, provided that the Rite of Unification were acknowledged to be a real ordination of those who had not previously been episcopally ordained. In both Convocations there was a strong group which objected to the two schemes on the ground of the validity of Anglican orders, and the invalidity of non-episcopal orders; a doctrine which had been firmly asserted in a volume of essays entitled *The Apostolic Ministry*, published in 1946 under the name of the late Bishop Kirk of Oxford, a volume in which I myself had a share.

I regret that this book has had to begin in this somewhat dismal way, with an account of debates in the Convocations which must appear to the outsider to be squabbles about ecclesiastical organization. But those who took part in them believed, and it will be the object of this book to show, that the problems then discussed do in fact go back in vital ways to the nature of the Christian Gospel itself, and therefore have a real relevance to the conflict in which all the Christian forces are engaged today with the secularism of a civilization which by and large has ceased to live by the Christian faith.

(ii) *The Episcopal Ministry*

I believe that *The Apostolic Ministry* was basically right in its positive affirmations, even though in the twenty-three years or so since the preparations for it began new issues have come up which call for fresh study of certain points, but that it was wrong in some of its negative implications, notably its rejection of all non-episcopal Ministries as invalid. This will bring us in a moment to the statement of a dilemma—the same that underlay those confused Convocation debates.

Let us start with the positive affirmation of the book. It was, that there really is such a thing as a basic shape or structure of Church Order, of which the Episcopal Ministry is the central point. It is true indeed, as several of the writers found occasion to say, that the Office of the Bishop has taken different forms at different periods, so that the present style of the Anglican episcopate in England cannot be taken as the standard pattern of it; thus, there are great differences between the pre-Nicene bishop and the missionary monk of the Dark Ages, and the mediaeval prelate, and the Hanoverian grandee, and the hard-worked pastor of today, and the missionary bishop among the Pacific islands, and a Japanese bishop in his own native land. Yet there is a continuity and unity in these various episcopacies, which depends on the nature of the office itself.

It has, however, been a common fault among us Anglicans to present the Episcopal Office as if it were primarily a matter of the Law and Constitution of the Church, and to fail to trace any special connection of it with the Gospel which our Lord proclaimed and entrusted to his Apostles. I think that it was a fault of *The Apostolic Ministry* too. Yet several years earlier the present Archbishop of Canterbury had written his book *The*

The Aim of this Book

Gospel and the Catholic Church. Nor did I make this point properly clear in 1954, when in re-writing the last chapter of my book *The Form of the Church* I set out a summary statement designed to show the many-sidedness of the Bishop's office. I shall endeavour to provide a more complete summary at the end of this present book. Yet even so, the old summary will be useful at this point:[1]

> Even now, we can see that the episcopal office represents the many-sidedness of the Apostolic function. It is not only, or chiefly, that the Bishop can exercise a juridical function in checking heretical teachings; but rather that his office covers and correlates with one another, not only sound doctrine, but evangelistic work, pastoral oversight of clergy and people, and the liturgical ministry of the sacraments, as no other form of ministerial office can ever do; while the fact that each Bishop is consecrated, not by his predecessor in the diocese, but by at least three other Bishops from outside it, signifies that his office is of a universal character, as was the Apostolate in its original institution, so that the Bishop represents his diocese in his relations with other bishops and dioceses, and represents them to it.

This summary is enough to show that the Bishop's office means much more than 'the Historic Episcopate', or 'a venerable form of church government'. But this book must start at once with the Gospel which our Lord proclaimed and the continuity of the Apostles' mission with his.

(iii) *A Dilemma*

Thus we have the episcopal office, glorious and wonderful indeed. But when everything is codified and expressed in a *doctrine* of episcopacy and in a Canon Law, it follows that the episcopal ministry is alone valid, and all non-episcopal ministries invalid, so that whatever of divine grace is mediated through them comes to be called 'uncovenanted mercies'. Such

[1] *The Form of the Church* (Faber, 1944), revised edition, 1954, p. 126.

A Dilemma

is the Roman Catholic system in its rigid form, where all is subordinated to the Pope. The Orthodox Churches of the East in general, and on the whole, regard the Orthodox Churches alone as the true Church, which alone has retained the fullness of the great tradition of worship and faith; but the Orthodox have very much to teach us of the West, lying as they do outside our Western tradition. Among Anglicans, the Tractarian revival of the doctrine of Valid Orders led to the formulation of the 'Branch Theory' of the Church, namely that the true Church is to be found wherever there is valid episcopacy in the apostolic succession. The positive claim here was that the Church of England was not merely a Protestant National Church, but a spiritual entity, part of the universal Church of God; that was in itself good and right. But the negative side of this claim was that all Christian societies which lacked episcopacy were thereby 'un-churched'; and this has aroused and arouses today a fierce and deep resentment.

This is one side of the matter. The other side is that it can scarcely be denied that our Lord does give his grace in non-episcopal sacraments, and that in non-episcopal churches the work of the Spirit has been manifest, producing real church life, and often setting a worthy pattern of the common life of believing and worshipping communities when an episcopal church had been signally failing to do so. Thus, it is not only that we read and profit today by the work of non-episcopal biblical scholars such as Dr. Dodd and the two Mansons or of theologians like Barth or the two Baillies—I am taking names at random—but also that in the life of their congregations non-episcopal churches have known better than we Anglicans how to assign to the laity their proper share. If clericalism was one of the sins of the middle ages, the Church of England at the Reformation did little to remedy this fault: a passive laity was still left under the control of the parson. But among the Presbyterians the *élite* of the laity became Elders and have borne a real share in the pastoral oversight of the congregation: indeed, for the laity as a whole the yoke of the Kirk Session became heavier than that of the unassisted parish priest. Among the Congregationalists there has been the Church Meeting, which at its best has been a truly wonderful instrument whereby the local church comes really to *be* the church. The same has been true of the Society of Friends, with their silent worship and the waiting of the Spirit for the spoken word to express thoughts that are in the mind of all. Among the Methodists, there has been the Class Meeting, which remained for a long time a most valuable instrument of spiritual fellowship, and there have been the Local Preachers, through whom a congregation accepts the responsibility of carrying on the ministry of prayer and preaching in the persons of some of its own members. Needless to say, it is easy to point out faults: but there are equally faults in the worship and the common life of Anglicans and Roman Catholics.

Here then is our dilemma. It is involved in holding, on the one side, that Episcopacy is right and is the proper form of the Church, and so that Episcopal Orders are 'valid', and on the other side acknowledging that there is authentic church life in the non-episcopal churches also. The dilemma is real: and it so turned out that within a month of the October meetings of the Convocations, when various speakers had given expression to the Anglo-Catholic doctrine of valid orders, there appeared an Open Letter by Thirty-two Theologians to the two Archbishops, the theme of which was that, since our Lord manifestly works through non-episcopal ministers of the Word and Sacraments, and episcopal ministries are also ministries of the Word and Sacraments, the episcopal and non-episcopal churches ought to recognize one another's ministries, and there should be Intercommunion: not only through the admission of non-episcopalians to Communion in the Church of England ('Open Communion'), but also that Anglicans should be prepared to receive Communion from non-episcopal ministers. There were faults, no doubt, in this letter, for conditions of intercommunion were not defined, and while the signatories did not desire indiscriminate intercommunion, they seemed to leave the door open for it. But anyway, the Open Letter vividly illustrated the dilemma of which we have spoken; and while this book will not answer this particular question, it will seek the principles which alone make a real answer possible.

Yet the dilemma is not a final one; for there is one Lord, one Gospel, one Body of Christ. A way will have been found out of it, when reunion shall have taken place. If all the Churches were to find their way to the reunion of all—a way such that in it all the partial truths for which the divided churches have contended were fully satisfied, so that the form and structure of 'Catholic' Christendom remained in being, with the sacramental and liturgical worship for which it exists, while at the same time full freedom was retained for the proclamation of the Gospel and the bringing forth of the fruits of the Spirit in the believing and worshipping community—when this shall have happened, the dilemma will have ceased to exist.

(iv) 'Static' and 'Dynamic' Views of the Church

It may further be noticed that the dilemma presupposes on either side a 'static' view of the Church. It was a static view of the Church which characterized the unhappy period after the Reformation and the persecutions and the wars of religion which followed it, when for centuries the various churches resembled fortresses, guarded by theologians who vigorously refuted one another's contentions.

But there were also movements of approach. On the Protestant side, there arose the Evangelical movement, which began with the Methodist preaching, but whose influence was widely felt outside Methodism. On the other side, the Anglo-Catholic movement with its Branch Theory which un-churched the Protestants, did open the way to a new knowledge of and sympathy with the devotional and liturgical life of the Roman Church and the Eastern Orthodox. The Anglo-Catholic movement was in its day a liturgical movement, for it was profoundly concerned with worship, but it tended to seek to return to the middle ages and idealize them.

In this century, however, there has been a Liturgical Movement which has sought to go back behind the middle ages to

The Aim of this Book

earlier patterns of Christian worship. This began in the Roman Church, but it was what the Church of England had intended to do from its Reformation onwards; and now it has spread among Presbyterians, Congregationalists, Baptists, Methodists and others in this country, and among Lutherans and Reformed on the Continent. This Liturgical Movement has been powerfully aided by the wonderful revival of Biblical Studies, which is now actively shared in by all the churches, including the Romans; we all read one another's books to our great profit. Together with this there has been the Ecumenical Movement, from the Edinburgh Conference of 1910 to that of New Delhi in 1961; and there is no place where the activities of the World Council of Churches are more closely and sympathetically followed than Rome.

Thus we have lately had from the Roman Church Professor Hans Küng's book *The Council and Reunion*[1] in which it is a main theme that the Church, being human as well as divine, is in constant need of reformation. Calvin, we remember, said the same. The Church has continually to be changing, while remaining the Church and retaining its continuity; but it must change because it is part of a world which is continually changing. It must change, in order to meet new situations, and it has done this repeatedly since its early days when it had to find Greek modes of expression for its Hebraic and biblical way of thought and life. But it retained its continuity; it spoke Greek, but it continued to think in an essentially biblical way. In our day, when incredibly great changes are taking place at a great speed, and when Asian and African nations are to be re-moulded by the Christian faith, the Church's outward shape must change, while it remains basically the same.

Such is the 'dynamic' view of the Church: and the word is, now as of old, 'He that hath an ear, let him hear what the Spirit saith unto the Churches'. The new Reformation both of the Reformation and the Counter-Reformation, which is now taking place, cannot be a return to the primitive church, or to the

[1] E. T. Sheed and Ward (1961); a paper-back, admirably translated by Cecily Hastings.

middle ages, or any other period which we may be tempted to idealize; it is never possible to put the clock back in that way. The return has always to be to the Gospel itself, to the Lord who once lived on earth and died and rose again, and who lives and reigns, and who, remaining the same, says, 'Behold, I make all things new'.

(v) *This Book and 'The Apostolic Ministry'*

Before starting on the main argument of this book, I must define the relation in which it is to stand to *The Apostolic Ministry*. The first thing to say is that a book of essays by several authors has the advantage that it can make full use of the specialist knowledge of authors on their own subjects, but the disadvantage that it cannot present a properly theological view of the whole subject, as a single author can attempt to do in thinking the whole subject through. We did indeed meet together for consultation many times, and we all saw one another's essays; but it was still a book by eleven authors. In this book I shall attempt to give a personal account of the whole subject as I see it, in relation to our situation today. The defects of my presentation of it will be apparent; my own studies have been mainly biblical and liturgical, and I cannot speak with authority as a church historian.

The Apostolic Ministry was undertaken over twenty years ago, and it was published in 1946. At that time most of us were very doubtful about the soundness of the scheme for church union in South India; since then, some of us who are still alive have come to take a much more favourable view of the South Indian Church, for much has happened in the Ecumenical Movement in these twenty years. Then again, new issues have come to the fore in regard to the problem of Faith and History, due largely to the work of Rudolf Bultmann; much of his chief writing had indeed already been published before 1940, but the problems which he raised had not then become a live issue in this country; here I speak for myself. If Bultmann is the typical heretic of our day, nevertheless he has asked many of the right questions, as will appear in the next chapter of this book. His great desire has been to present the Christian Gospel in a form in which it can be intelligible to the men of our day, and to learn how to speak to them in their language. But it does appear that in doing so he has missed that central point of the Christian Gospel, which is, in the words of 1 John 4.2, 'Jesus Christ come in the flesh'; in the gospels we have an authentic picture of the Jesus of history, and he who died on the cross is risen from the dead. Today the student of the gospels is compelled to face up to this problem. Hence my next chapter must deal with Faith and History, and the following one with the Call of the Twelve by Jesus, which Bultmann and some others call in question.

What was the Apostolic Commission? What was its relation to the Gospel which Jesus proclaimed? The New Testament answers to such questions are very different indeed from any answer which starts from the notion that our Lord was the Founder of a new Religion. If that were so, St. Paul and St. John could be expected to develop the New Religion on lines markedly different from those of its Founder, much as Aristotle who could be called a disciple of Plato made great changes in what he had learnt from Plato. Was it not on such lines as this that the Liberal Theology of half a century ago worked out its view of St. Paul? Jesus had proclaimed certain universal religious truths, the Fatherhood of God, the Brotherhood of Man, and the Infinite Value of the Human Soul; but Paul radically altered this simple message into a doctrine of Salvation from Sin, and John coming after him translated the whole into Hellenistic terms. Assertions such as these seem fantastic to us now; and the basic presupposition of such assertions was that Jesus was the Founder of a Religion. But the New Testament is free from any such presupposition.

Our book was criticized for the use which was made of the word *shaliach*, which is the Aramaic original of the Greek word *apostolos*. It was pointed out for instance that a Jewish *shaliach* could never appoint a deputy, and so, if the Apostles were *shelichim*, they could never have any successors.[1] Possibly our book laid itself open to this by its stress on the Jewish word; but if there was a fault, I believe it was that we did not adequately show the very great and deep difference between an ordinary *shaliach* and an apostle of Jesus, by presenting a study of the Gospel-message which he proclaimed, and the relation of the Apostolic Preaching to that. The result would have been to show that in this unique case the *shelichim* of Jesus must have successors.

Finally, I feel bound to criticize *The Apostolic Ministry* for the fault, for which I share responsibility, of saying little about the Reformation itself and its effort to remedy the faults of the mediaeval church. We ought in our historical survey to have dealt with Luther's proclamation of the Gospel, and with the questions which he left partly unanswered about the episcopal ministry and priesthood, and about sacrifice and the Eucharist; for it was not right to leave the treatment of the whole problem of Protestantism to a brief sketch by Bishop Mackenzie, coming after our historical survey had been completed. I shall therefore attempt to deal with these questions in this book, and with the theology of the laity implied in the 'Priesthood of All Christians'. This will bring us to a concluding chapter about the non-episcopal Ministries and the meaning of the Episcopal Office.

[1] A. Ehrhardt, *The Apostolic Succession*, London (1953), p. 20; A. Hanson, *The Pioneer Ministry*, SCM (1961), pp. 9–10, and others.

CHAPTER II

The Historical Jesus

★

The idea of an Apostolic Ministry demands a study of history; the idea of an Apostolic Succession brings up the thought of nineteen centuries of history since the days of the Apostles, and demands a historical study which must begin with the gospels. The modern study of the gospels has raised in an acute form the problem of Faith and History. In this chapter, then, we will deal with the problem in the gospels, and in the next start with the question raised by Rudolf Bultmann whether Jesus really called the Twelve; for he holds that this is a belief which first arose in the primitive church and has no foundation in history. The basic question is, then, whether an honest study of history is really possible for those who accept a creed which makes dogmatic assertions about certain historical events.

(i) *The Christian Faith*

No other world-religion is tied to history as the Christian faith is, except the faith of Israel out of which it sprang. We believe, as Israel has believed, that the One God, the maker of heaven and earth, has revealed himself in history, in his mighty acts of Salvation and Judgement. In the Old Testament, the typical act of Salvation is the LORD's deliverance of Israel out of Egypt in the Exodus, and his Covenant with them at Sinai; and the typical act of Judgement is the Fall of Jerusalem in 587 B.C., when he allowed his chosen people to be uprooted from the promised land, their temple to be destroyed, and their political existence extinguished. Yet this act of Judgement was interpreted by the prophets as the prelude to a future work of Salvation; for it was evident that if the LORD was chastizing them for their sins, he had not finished his purpose with them. There would yet be an anointed King, a son of David, exercising world-wide dominion. There would be a second Exodus and a new Covenant with an outpouring of God's Spirit, and all nations would come in to share in the knowledge of God which Israel had learnt.

The New Testament rests on the announcement of the Gospel or Good News that this promised divine action has taken place, in the person of Jesus the Messiah or Anointed King. He had proclaimed that God's Hour of Salvation and Judgement had struck; 'The Kingdom of God', he said, 'is upon you' (Mark 1.15); and when Israel had quailed at this challenging message, and had rejected him and seen him brought to the terrible death of crucifixion, God had raised him from the dead and vindicated him as Lord and Messiah (Acts 2.36). And now, by his resurrection and the gift of the messianic Spirit, men were made sharers by baptism in the New Covenant, sharers in his death and in his risen life; and this was not for Israelites only, but also for people of all nations.

If we try to express the essential Christian faith in phrases such as the original apostles and evangelists might have used, it comes out somewhat thus:[1]

(a) The Good News which Jesus proclaimed was true; the Kingdom of God really was breaking in.

(b) God had sent Jesus to say what he said, and do what he did, and suffer what he suffered; for God was fulfilling in him his purpose of Salvation and Judgement which he had begun with the call of Abraham and the Exodus under Moses, and which he had caused to be interpreted to Israel by the prophets.

(c) When Israel rejected Jesus and brought him to the death

[1] This is set out at length in Chapter VIII of my book *The Christ of Faith and the Jesus of History*, S.C.M. Press (1962), pp. 101–21.

25

of the cross, God, reversing that sentence, raised him from the dead.

(d) Who then is he? He is the Messiah, the Son of God.

Such would be the answer of faith. Opponents would acknowledge the public facts of his preaching and his death, but would say that God had not sent him, he was not the Messiah, and of course did not rise from the dead.

(ii) *Faith and History*

The problem of Faith and History was, then, an actual problem from the beginning. In our own day it has become specially acute, since we are now able to pursue the study of the history of the past with far greater thoroughness and much fuller knowledge of the events of that past than was ever possible before; and we are confronted with a dilemma from which it is not easy to escape. It can be stated thus:

On the one hand, when we affirm the faith which the Apostles of Jesus believed, we are affirming as they did that God's saving action has happened within history; the events did happen, and are factually true. It seems, then, that we already possess the answers to the questions which the historian must investigate; and if the answers are given beforehand, how can there be any genuine historical inquiry?

This can readily be illustrated from the field of biblical studies. There are those for whom the affirmation that 'the Bible is true' means that everything recorded in the Bible is factually true; the Book of Daniel, for instance, must have been written by a Daniel who was taken into exile from Jerusalem in 597 or else 587 B.C., and the Pastoral Epistles which claim to have been written by St. Paul were actually composed by him. If, as very many scholars hold, these books were not written by Daniel and St. Paul respectively, the book would be making a false claim, and the Bible would not be true. Hence the faithful Christian ought to read the works of 'conservative' scholars only, which reach the required results. On this view there is no real freedom of research. In its extreme form, such a view would require us to hold that Methuselah really did live to the age of 969, Balaam's ass really did speak with a human voice, and so on; otherwise the Bible is not true.

But the problem is a real one for us all. If it were demonstrated beyond all doubt that Jesus never lived, and the records of him are entirely mythical, our faith would be at an end. This view is held by no one now. But equally, if Jesus did not rise from the dead, our faith would be at an end; and here there are distinguished scholars, such as Bultmann, who hold that the most that the historian can affirm is that his disciples believed that he was risen. This however is very different from what St. Paul affirms in 1 Cor. 15, that Jesus Christ did in fact rise from the dead, and 'if Christ was not raised, then our Gospel is null and void, and so is your faith; and we turn out to be lying witnesses for God' (I Cor. 15.14–15). We will return to consider the Resurrection later in this chapter; here we are stating the problem.

On the other hand, when we affirm the freedom of historical inquiry and research, is it the case that all the affirmations of faith must be left as open questions till the historians have finished investigating them? If so, are we not at the mercy of the historians, and does not the last word lie with them? We have appealed to history, and to history we must go. But then, since historical evidence is often incomplete, there are degrees of probability in the results which can be reached. In many cases there is actual certainty. No one doubts that on D-Day, 6th June 1944, the allied forces effected a successful landing on the coast of France, or that Julius Caesar was assassinated at Rome on 15th March in 43 B.C. or again that Jesus of Nazareth was crucified at Jerusalem at Passover time in some year not long before or after A.D. 30. Many other events are probable but not certain, because of defective evidence, as for instance whether St. Peter and St. Paul were executed at Rome in A.D. 64. Is faith, then, to rest on the historians' verdict, a verdict which may well be 'Not proven'? But faith needs firm ground on which to rely.

The actual problem with regard to the gospel-story which

stands at the centre of the Christian faith, is this. It is admitted
that the gospels, as we have them, were written a whole generation at least after the events which they describe, and were
written by Christian evangelists for Christian readers. The
public for which they were written was then a very different
public from that to which Jesus is declared to have preached,
namely to the crowds in Galilee or Jerusalem, to the Pharisees,
to his own disciples. Would not the word which the early
Christians needed be different from that which his original
hearers needed? Again, he proclaimed the Gospel of the Kingdom of God; but, as Bultmann very rightly says, after the
resurrection the Proclaimer became the Proclaimed One, for the
apostles proclaimed Jesus, that he was the Son of God. Can
then the evangelists' record have been 'coloured' by their faith
in him and their belief about him? It would indeed be natural
and fitting that the narratives should have been thus 'coloured'
to some extent, if the evangelists were thinking all the time *both*
of the remembered acts and words of Jesus, *and* of him as the
risen Lord, the object of faith and worship to them and to their
readers.

But the problem becomes really acute when we see that
responsible scholars like Martin Dibelius and Bultmann have
been denying that there were 'remembered' acts and words of
Jesus, and asserting that the evangelists' faith and the Church's
faith have coloured the gospels to such an extent that they do
in fact tell us very much about the life and thought of the
apostolic church, but very little that is historically reliable about
the Jesus of the ministry. This is almost to say that the Jesus
of the gospels is a 'mythical Christ'; and it recalls what we said
a page or two back about attempts to prove that he never
existed, since it comes to much the same thing if he did exist
but we know next to nothing about him.

Yet, since the object of historical research is to find out the
truth, we cannot forbid such a study or refuse to engage in it.
For there is a truth about the events, just as there is a truth
which faith seeks to apprehend. Here are two truths, or rather
two sorts of truth. And our problem arises out of the affirmation

of Christian faith, that both sorts of truth are involved in the answer.

Have we not here the clue to the answer? For myself, I feel that I owe a great debt to Prof. Helmut Gollwitzer, of West Berlin, for working this point out clearly,[1] and showing that the Christian who wants to believe that Jesus is the Son of God, and also wants to take the appeal to history seriously, may take encouragement from the fact that exactly this problem is involved in the affirmation that 'the Word was made flesh and dwelt among us'. When the Son of God was made man, he became subject to the observation of men, and to men of all sorts, both godly and ungodly. Men could watch him doing his work, and hear what he said and did, and describe what he said and did. Some might do this faithfully, having really tried to understand and to obey; others might misunderstand and misrepresent what they had seen and heard, through carelessness and inattentiveness, or again through resentment at what he did and said, and their resentment might amount to a malicious hostility. To all this the Son of God would necessarily become subject in being made man; and this is what the gospels record.

We feel sure that we are reading authentic records of what Jesus said and did, related by intelligent witnesses and faithfully handed down, when we read such inimitable parables as those of the Good Samaritan or the Prodigal Son, or the account in Luke 7.36–50 of a dinner in the house of Simon the Pharisee. Yet even faithful disciples could misunderstand what his real word to them was, as when in Mark 8.31–3 Peter rejected his first prediction of his passion, or in 10.37 James and John sought for themselves chief places in the coming Kingdom. It was a different and a very radical misunderstanding when some of the religious leaders could look on him restoring epileptics to health and mentally-diseased persons to sanity—for

---

[1] In a paper which appeared in *Theology*, March 1962, with the title 'The Jesus of History and Faith in Jesus Christ', translated from the original in *Der historische Jesus und der kerygmatische Christus*, ed. H. Ristow and K. Matthiae, Evangelische Verlagsanstalt, Berlin (1960), pp. 110–14.

these are the outward and visible symptoms of demon-possession as the gospels describe them—and say that when he cast out devils it was because he was in league with Beelzebul the prince of the devils. Here was a conflict as acute as it well could be; for he on his part was saying, 'If it is by the finger of God that I cast out devils, then be sure that the Kingdom of God has already come upon you' (Luke 11.20).

He had come among men with a challenge, and the challenge was being rejected. He proclaimed that God's Hour had struck, the Hour of the coming Kingdom, and he confronted men with the present call of God, to believe that it was true, and to repent. It was a word with authority; those whom he called to be disciples must leave all and follow him. He went to sick people who could not help themselves; and when he said, 'The blind recover their sight, the lame walk, the lepers are clean, the deaf hear, the dead are raised, and the poor hear the Good News of salvation', he was echoing the words of Isa. 35.5–6 and 61.1, describing the blessings that God would give his people in the future Day of Deliverance. He went to tax-gatherers and sinners, the non-respectable and outcast, who likewise needed help; for as he said, 'It is not the healthy who need a doctor, but the sick; I did not come to invite virtuous people, but sinners' (Mark 2.17).

It was his mission to taxgatherers and sinners which seems to have provoked more than anything else the resentment of the religious leaders; for was he not undoing the patient work of the Scribes in the synagogues, who were always exhorting the people to keep the Law and lead moral lives? His whole way of approach was deeply shocking to those for whom the observance of all the rules was a primary duty; and for his part, such figures as the Elder Brother in the parable of the Prodigal Son, or the Pharisee in that of the Pharisee and the Publican, indicate that he saw the self-righteousness of the godly as a far more serious problem than the flagrant offences of the 'sinners'.

So then: His Gospel-message was proclaimed to all, and all could observe what he said and did; but while some were receptive to his mission and message, others were scandalized

Faith and History

and aroused to fury, such fury that in the end he was brought to death by crucifixion. As he said, the things of God were revealed to the simple, but hidden from the wise and learned (Matt. 11.25). Or we can put the same point in the language of the later church theology, and say that while the humanity of Jesus was observable by all, his divine nature could be discerned only by the spiritually responsive.

This spiritual responsiveness is faith; for faith is not merely *belief that* Jesus was sent by God and was the Son of God, but *personal response to him* and self-committal to him. Mere orthodoxy of belief is not necessarily faith. So we return to our problem of Faith and History. The historian is professionally concerned with the records of the events which happened and the evidence for them, so that he must compare what is said in one gospel with what is said in another, and draw his conclusions; and what he says must be attended to. He is not concerned, *qua* historian, with the spiritual issues, for his first duty is to deal truly with the evidence; but *as a man* he is confronted with the same spiritual issues with which every man is confronted who hears the Gospel. He also must either stay and listen, or turn away. And the answer which he gives to this central Question will necessarily affect the way in which he writes his history.

We may then formulate a provisional answer to our problem. The Christian faith is tied to history; hence we may not affirm belief in historical facts which we do honestly think to be true, and we need the historian's research. But we who believe that the Christian faith is true cannot expect to be able to demonstrate to the satisfaction of non-Christians that the interpretations which we give of the gospels are historically correct.[1] It is our duty to be entirely faithful to the evidence, and not to make assertions which we cannot justify to ourselves, and to be prepared to find that a non-Christian scholar may have perceived some points which we had missed. But we have a right to make affirmations, as for instance with regard to our Lord's resurrection, which we cannot demonstrate to those who do not share

[1] See the text and the footnote on pp. 53–4.

31

our faith. This principle applies also to the critical investigation
of the origins of Episcopacy.

(iii) *The Resurrection on the Third Day*

On the affirmation that Jesus of Nazareth rose again from
the dead all Christian faith depends; at the same time the
historical problem is here notoriously difficult. That in itself
might be a sufficient reason for a discussion of it here. But we
need to speak of it also because it is the point from which the
Apostolic mission starts, and on it all the history of the Church
depends.

The Church's faith in the Resurrection rests upon the testimony of the Apostles, who are repeatedly spoken of in the Acts
as 'witnesses' to it, and whose testimony is given in 1 Cor. 15.
They believed that he was risen, in spite of the fact that he had
been crucified; for crucifixion was not merely a peculiarly
horrible and shameful form of execution, but it was also in the
eyes of every Jew an accursed death. In Gal. 3.13 St. Paul
alludes to the belief which he himself had formerly held, that
Jesus the Crucified was the Accursed One, when he quotes the
text from Deut. 21.23, 'Cursed is everyone who is hanged on a
tree'. So in 1 Cor. 12.3 he speaks of some who call Jesus
accursed, and these are the Jews; for every Jew would say,
when he heard how Jesus had died that he was proved thereby
to be not God's Blessed One, the Messiah and 'the King of the
Jews', but an Accursed One, condemned by the voice of God's
high priest and the supreme council of the Sanhedrin, and
indeed by God himself who had allowed this dreadful thing to
happen. It is possible and even probable that Caiaphas had
planned to bring about his death by crucifixion and not some
other way, in order to provide the whole nation with this
demonstration of the falsehood of his Gospel-message.

The apostles were Jews, and this terrible negative demonstration was the first thing that their faith had to overcome. To
affirm that he was risen was to say that God had wiped out the
curse and had reversed the sentence of men upon him; and this

is what we are told in Acts 4.5–10, that they spoke to Caiaphas and the whole Jewish hierarchy of 'Jesus Christ of Nazareth, whom you crucified, whom God raised from the dead'. Yet they themselves had failed most wretchedly on the night of his passion; they had all forsaken him and fled, and Peter had publicly disowned him. They themselves must have been broken men on that Good Friday night, men out of whose lives faith and hope had gone; all that they had believed in and lived for must have seemed to be proved false, and they themselves had failed him at the last. Something had happened to cause the change from despair to courageous faith, which certainly took place; and one reason for thinking that the First Epistle of Peter really is his, is that the first words of the epistle after the usual salutation seem exactly to fit Peter's experience:

'Praise be to the God and Father of our Lord Jesus Christ, who in his mercy gave us new birth into a living hope by the resurrection of Jesus Christ from the dead' (1 Peter 1.3); into 'a living hope', when faith and hope had died, into 'a new birth', a new life out of death. He was risen, and they were risen too; they had become new men.

There were Appearances; they saw him risen; as the earliest written testimony says, 'He appeared to Cephas, and afterwards to the Twelve. Then he appeared to over five hundred of our brothers at once, most of whom are still alive, though some have died' (1 Cor. 15.5–6). The appearance to Peter is put as the first. It is one of the remarkable things about St. Mark's gospel, in which Peter is prominent throughout and which must at the very least contain some of his memories, that the appearance to Peter, to which the narrative seems to be leading up, is not described. Perhaps the simplest explanation is right, that it was such that no third person could attempt to describe it.

But did the Easter faith of the apostles rest only on the appearance of the Lord to them? If they were cross-questioned, as they must have been, it was always possible for the other side to say, 'You had visions of Jesus as risen; but we have had no such experiences, and you have no accounts to give of the risen

Jesus being thus seen by any except believers.' The apostles could not prove that the appearances were more than visions; and so they would be thought of by any outsider. Caiaphas himself would surely have found no difficulty in thinking that the disciples of Jesus had seen visions; and Bultmann today, who says that the historians can go no further than to affirm that the disciples believed that he was risen, is not, perhaps, in very good company.

The apostles however affirmed that Jesus *was* risen: 'God raised him from the dead'; the resurrection was a real Event. It was not indeed an event that could be described, and the gospels make no attempt to do so. 'That which happened' in the resurrection of Jesus was and remains God's own secret. Yet if the apostles' testimony was testimony to an Event, to a real fact, and not merely to experiences which they had had, it would be right and fitting that there should be some piece of brute fact such as an unexplained disappearance of a body which had been buried, so that the tomb was found empty. Such a piece of brute fact could stand as an outward and visible sign of the divine action. All the four gospels contain the narrative of the Empty Tomb; and the same ought surely to be taken to be implied in the official formula in 1 Cor. 15.3–4:

'Christ died—for our sins—according to the Scriptures—and was buried; and was raised—on the third day—according to the Scriptures—and was seen . . .'

That which was buried was raised; the body was raised. A miracle? Yes indeed, a miracle; for *if* the Gospel which Jesus proclaimed was true, and God had sent him to proclaim and bring to men the Kingdom of God, a direct Action of God is fitting at this, the central point of human history. When the Son of God had come into the world, and sinful and self-centred Man had turned on him and killed him, it is fitting that God himself should vindicate his Son, by such an outward and visible sign.

But someone will say, 'Is not such a Sign out of place? Would it not be a demonstration by factual evidence, which would prove the Lord's resurrection to be true on the level of scientific knowledge, and put it on a level with verifiable events such as the murder of Julius Caesar?' This can sound reasonable, till we ask, '*To whom* is the demonstration offered? To Caiaphas? Caiaphas would soon learn that the disciples of Jesus believed that his tomb had been found empty; and we can easily see what his reaction would be. He would reply, 'Rubbish! His disciples came by night and stole the body while we were asleep.' These words are a quotation from Matthew 28.13, where we read two verses later that 'this story became widely known, and is current in Jewish circles to this day'. Similarly, does the so-called demonstration convince secularists and humanists today? Sometimes the narrative is accepted, and is explained in ingenious ways, as that in Mark 16.5–6 the Young Man at the tomb was trying to tell the women that they had come to the wrong tomb, and saying, 'He is not *here*; look, *there* is the place where they laid him', and the hysterical women jumped to a wrong conclusion, and so the whole error began. Or Joseph of Arimathaea removed the body and told no one, and presumably left Jerusalem and never returned. Or there was an earthquake, and the body disappeared in a crack which opened in the rock. The reader can judge what these theories are worth; and probably he will be more prepared to respect those who say that the whole story is a legend which arose because the disciples, being Jews, could not conceive of resurrection otherwise than as the re-animation of the body. But there it is. When the Sign is offered as a demonstration to those who do not believe that God was in Christ reconciling the world to himself, we find that the demonstration does not convince them.

This is not to say that if we accept the Sign our problems are all solved. In the stories of the Appearances of the risen Lord, he is never described as simply *returning* to the life that he had lived during his ministry, as those who according to the gospel accounts were raised to life by him returned to their former manner of life, so that they would die again when their time came. The risen Lord is different; he appears in a room where the doors are shut, and he vanishes out of their sight; we are not led to think of him as living *in some place* between the various appearances, nor of *walking back* invisibly to Jerusalem from Emmaus that he may appear there. It is *the same* Jesus, for all the accounts emphasize this; but he is different, he is transformed. Similarly in the latter part of 1 Cor. 15 St. Paul explains that for us also the future resurrection-body must be a 'glorified' body, a 'spiritual' body (v. 44); for 'flesh and blood can never possess the Kingdom of God, and the perishable cannot possess immortality' (v. 50). In both cases, the two key-words are *continuity* and *transformation*. Our thought is baffled here; but we can take comfort from the thought that the difficulty comes in the right place, at the point where our thought is bound to be baffled anyhow. That point is, the relation between human life under the conditions of this world and human life in the world beyond death. So it is when our Lord passes beyond death. 'That which happened' is and remains God's secret. But it can be right for the secret thing, the mystery, to be represented by an outward and visible Sign, a Miracle, in the unexplained disappearance from the tomb of the body which was known to have been buried. And the Apostles did believe that the tomb was found empty.

Let us, then, be as critical as we like, as critical as we can. It could be that some of the points which come up in the resurrection-narratives are the products of the Church's faith; thus, there may well be in St. Luke a tendency to materialize the picture that he draws of the risen Lord, in order that he may make it quite clear to his Greek readers that the whole Christian doctrine of resurrection is of a resurrection of the body, as opposed to the pagan Greek idea of the survival of an immortal 'soul'. But the final issue is the question which is addressed to every one who hears the Gospel-message, whether he will believe that the Gospel which Jesus proclaimed was true, and that God had sent him and God was accomplishing in him his purpose for the salvation of mankind, and that when men rejected Jesus and crucified him God raised him from the dead.

Thus the Christian Faith is necessarily tied to history, and therefore must be studied by scientific historical methods, and the things which are said by non-Christian or imperfectly-Christian scholars must be seriously attended to, as well as the things which are said by orthodox scholars. We need to know the truth about the verifiable historical facts. But the Gospel also demands a personal response on the part of all to whom it is proclaimed; and the Christian claim is that faith alone gives the right clue to the interpretation of the factual evidence, whereas unbelief lacks the clue and will misinterpret the evidence, and misunderstand the testimony of the Apostles that Jesus rose from the dead. The continuation of the Apostles' message throughout church history is what we are to study in this book.

CHAPTER III

Jesus and the Apostles

★

The most important point in this chapter is the continuity between the Gospel message which Jesus proclaimed and that which the Apostles preached after his resurrection.[1] But it is necessary to begin with the Call of the Twelve by Jesus, distinguishing the Twelve from the other Apostles.

When *The Apostolic Ministry* was being written between 1940 and 1945, we all, I think, were sure that this was a certain fact. But today it is being questioned; for since the Apostles filled a large place in the life of the primitive church, it is asked whether the very idea of apostleship did not first arise within the primitive church, and then was read back into the period of the ministry of Jesus. So for instance Bultmann says that 'Paul calls all missionaries apostles (1 Cor. 9.5; Rom. 16.7; 2 Cor. 11.5, 13; 12.11 ff.)';[2] and with regard to the call of the Twelve by our Lord, he says, 'The less likely it is that the Twelve were called by Jesus himself, the more characteristic they are for the eschatological consciousness of the Church: for they are "the Twelve" not as the apostles but as the eschatological regents.'[3] The reference here is to Matt. 19.28, Luke 22.29 f., where it is promised that they shall 'sit on thrones as judges of the twelve tribes of Israel'.

---

[1] See p. 45 below.
[2] Bultmann, *Theology of the New Testament*, I, p. 60.
[3] ibid., p. 37.

The Twelve

(i) *The Twelve*

We must consider 'the Twelve' first, for this designation of the Twelve Disciples belongs to the narratives of the ministry, whereas in the post-resurrection period there were other 'Apostles' besides them. Here Günther Bornkamm can speak very definitely, making reference to Bultmann's thesis.[1]

'The importance and the task of discipleship is symbolically represented by the number of twelve disciples whom Jesus appoints: "And he appointed twelve, to be with him, and to be sent out to preach, and have authority to cast out demons" (Mark 3.14 f.). The twelve disciples are scarcely the creation of the post-Easter Church, as has been suggested, though they had certainly a representative significance in the earliest years. Their institution certainly goes back to the historical Jesus, because the fact that Judas Iscariot belonged to their circle was a serious stumbling-block to the later Church. We also learn from the oldest source about the appearance of the Resurrected Lord, quoted by Paul in 1 Cor. 15.3 ff., that he appeared to the Twelve (*den Zwölfen*).[2] Their circle must therefore have existed before Easter. The number twelve symbolises the twelve tribes of Israel (Matt. 19.28; Luke 22.30). Jesus' disciples were thus conceived as the new people of God of the last days. This is however not to be understood in the sense of the "holy remnant" of the righteous,[3] and is not true in the sense of any isolation from Israel, but is the

---

[1] Bornkamm, *Jesus of Nazareth*, p. 150 (in the German original, p. 138).

[2] The English translation here wrongly omits the word 'the', and reads 'to twelve disciples'.

[3] I am persuaded that Bornkamm is right here in denying that the Twelve were intended to be 'the Remnant', for the reason which he states here and develops further on his pp. 43 (39) and 77–8 (70–1); Jesus' disciples were not a holy sect like the Essenes, and he himself went to the 'taxgatherers and sinners'. The thesis that the Twelve were the Remnant is the governing idea of *The Pioneer Ministry*, by A. T. Hanson, SCM (1961), where a view of the Christian Ministry is developed which is very different from mine. I have given on pp. 42–3 what seems to me to be a decisive refutation of the thesis that the Twelve were the Remnant.

Jesus and the Apostles

visible symbol of Jesus' call, which goes out to the lost sheep of the house of Israel (Matt. 10.6; 15.24).'

Here are two good reasons. It would not have been a matter of great concern if the betrayer had been one of an undefined group of those who had followed Jesus; but Judas was 'ὁ εἷς τῶν δώδεκα', Mark 14.10.[1] If the idea of 'the Twelve' had first arisen in the apostolic age, no list of the Twelve would have included his name. The second reason is equally cogent: for 1 Cor. 15.5 is the only place where the term 'the Twelve' occurs in the New Testament outside the Gospels, except Acts 6.2. It occurs in the earliest quasi-credal formulary, which St. Paul had 'received' and which he had 'delivered' to the Church at Corinth. From whom had he received it? It is possible, and probable, that he had received it from Peter, when, three years after his conversion, he went to Jerusalem 'to get to know Peter'; for the Greek is ἱστορῆσαι Κεφᾶν, and the word ἱστορεῖν denotes questioning, inquiry, investigation. He went to Peter, among other things, for much-needed information.

There seems to be no reason to question the Mission of the Twelve during the ministry (Mark 6.7 ff. etc.). It can well be that the Mission of the Seventy (or Seventy-two) is a duplicate of this, for while Matthew makes one mission only, in his ch. 10, Luke makes two missions, keeping his Markan source and his Q-source separate. Dr. Austin Farrer suggested in *The Apostolic Ministry* (pp. 135–8) that to Luke the Seventy (or Seventy-two, according to the same good MSS., reckoning in Eldad and Medad) recalled the 70 Elders or Presbyters of Numbers 11. Luke had in his mind the mission of the Twelve (Apostles) in the first generation of church history, but by the time he wrote their work was mostly over: hence he treated in greater detail the mission of the Seventy, because an increasing responsibility was resting upon presbyters in his day.

Bornkamm writes of the Mission of the Twelve:

'The disciples are thus not only the recipients of the healing powers of the coming Kingdom of God, those powers which

---

[1] Why does St. Mark use the article here? Does he mean '*that* one of the Twelve who . . .' ?

are already present and mighty in Jesus' word and deed; rather, they are most actively drawn into the service of his message and the proclamation of the Kingdom's victory (Mark 3.14 f.; Luke 10.17 ff.). We have certainly to take into account the fact that the descriptions of the disciples, their commission and inspired deeds, have been coloured by the experiences of the early church. But this by no means excludes the fact that the historical Jesus made his disciples share in his authority. It is easy to understand in this connection that the question of a special reward could arise among them: a very human question, it is true, but one which Jesus strictly forbids them, as is shown in his answer to the request made by the sons of Zebedee (Mark 10.35 ff.).'[1]

(ii) *The Apostles*

As has been said, the title 'the Twelve' does not occur outside the Gospels, except in 1 Cor. 15.5 and in Acts 6.2 where 'the Seven' are about to be appointed. But there are other 'Apostles' besides them; Paul, Barnabas, James the Lord's brother, perhaps Silas (as 1 Thess. 2.7 strongly suggests), and seemingly Andronicus and Junias, mentioned in Rom. 16.7 as having been Christians before St. Paul's conversion. Was it that they were the founders of the Church at Rome?

It is, however, simply not true that, as Bultmann says, 'Paul calls all missionaries apostles'. The word *apostolos* is used twice (though the English versions all translate it otherwise) to mean 'a delegate' (*shaliach*) appointed by some local church for some special purpose. Thus Epaphroditus in Phil. 2.25 is the 'apostle' of the Philippian congregation sent to minister to St. Paul's needs; and in 2 Cor. 8.23 there are two unnamed ἀπόστολοι ἐκκλησιῶν, officially appointed by unnamed churches, as is described in 8.19, to be in charge of those churches' share in the Collection being made for Jerusalem. This same office of *shaliach* is alluded to also in 1 Cor. 16.3-4, of those whom the Corinthians will elect for the same purpose. It is possible that

[1] op. cit., p. 149 (German text, pp. 137–8).

the list in Acts 20.4 (Sopater of Beroea, Aristarchus and Secundus of Thessalonica, Gaius and Timothy of Derbe, Tychicus and Trophimus of the province of Asia) are some of these 'apostles of Churches' for this purpose. *Shaliach* here implies a temporary delegation of authority for a temporary duty; this is its regular Jewish use.

But the word 'apostle' in its regular use in the New Testament means 'an apostle of Jesus Christ' (so in the opening words of 1 Cor., 2 Cor., Eph., Col., and 1 Timothy, 2 Timothy, Titus); 'an apostle, not by human appointment or human commission, but by commission from the Lord Jesus Christ and from God the Father who raised him from the dead', Gal. 1.1;[1] and so, in the latter part of 2 Corinthians he speaks in 10.8 of 'an authority given by the Lord to build you up, not pull you down', and the same phrase, word for word the same in the Greek text, in 13.10, right at the end. He speaks of 'those who were apostles before me', Gal. 1.17; and in 1 Cor. 9.1 he says, 'Am I not an apostle? Have I not seen Jesus our Lord?'

This suggests that in 1 Cor. 15.7 the term 'all the apostles' refers to Barnabas and others who had received the Lord's call in the period after Easter; each one of them had 'seen the Lord'.[2] The certified list in vv. 5 ff. is first Cephas, then the Twelve, then five hundred or more, then James, then 'all the apostles', and last Paul himself. If so, 'all the apostles' means, not the Twelve at the Ascension, but 'each one who received the Lord's personal call'; and the list of the Apostles was a closed list, even though we do not know for certain who were included in it.

The evidence that we have cited already tells strongly against the view that the Apostles were during the ministry 'the Church-in-embryo', or that they constituted the 'Remnant'; as in the words of F. J. A. Hort, 'In virtue of the personal faith vivifying their discipleship, the Apostles became themselves the first little Ecclesia, constituting a living rock upon which a far larger and

---

[1] This proves that the laying-on of hands in Acts 13.3 was not an ordination.

[2] So Austin Farrer suggests, in *The Apostolic Ministry*, pp. 125–30.

ever enlarging Ecclesia would shortly be built up';[1] and A. C. Headlam later held a similar view.[2] The clearest evidence that the Apostles were from the beginning a group within a community is that of 1 Cor. 15.5: the Lord appeared after Easter to the Twelve, and then to the Five Hundred, who are designated as 'brethren'. This figure of 500 is in accord with the testimony of Acts 1.15 that those of them who were in Jerusalem in the days before Pentecost were about 120.

Thus there was already a fairly large circle of 'brethren', with the Apostles at the centre. The truth for which that other view stands is that the Apostolate and the later Christian Ministry must never be thought of in separation from the Church; we shall return to this point frequently. But the evidence does show that the Apostles had a definite place of their own within the Church from the beginning.

(iii) *The Apostolic Commission*

For what was an 'Apostle of Jesus' commissioned? What was he to be, what was he to do, what message was he to give? To answer these questions we must go back to consider the mission and message of Jesus himself.

Nowhere in the gospels do we find the least suggestion or hint that Jesus ever conferred with his disciples or consulted them about his mission or about what he should say or do next. He speaks with them very often, but always either to instruct and teach them, or to reprove the faults which often are apparent. In a quite extraordinary way he stands alone.[3] Sometimes indeed he is spoken of as a prophet. Yet he never provides authority for his message as a prophet in the Old Testament felt bound to do, by describing his call to be a prophet, or by the use of such formula as 'Thus saith the Lord',

[1] F. J. A. Hort, *The Christian Ecclesia*, p. 17, cf. 32, 167.
[2] A. C. Headlam, *The Doctrine of the Church and Christian Reunion* (Bampton Lectures, 1920), p. 37. I owe these two references to A. T. Hanson, *The Pioneer Ministry*, pp. 137 and 142.
[3] For the rest of this paragraph, *see* Bornkamm, *Jesus of Nazareth*, pp. 56 ff., or in the German original, pp. 51 ff.

or 'the word of the Lord came to me, saying'. He speaks with an immediate authority of God's present call to men. He is regularly addressed as 'Rabbi' or 'Teacher', and so he preaches in synagogues, and engages with rabbis in argument; but he is different. His parables are unlike those of the rabbis, which are mere illustrations of their formal teaching; his parables *are* his teaching, for they are drawn directly from life, and sketch out some situation concerning which the hearer is frequently asked to give his judgement, and draw his own conclusions. Or again, while the rabbi would base his teaching on an exegesis of some scriptural text, supported by the Tradition of the Elders, Jesus never does this: he speaks of the Kingdom of God in its immediate and present application, and it is in this context that he quotes Scripture. He declares the call of God to his hearers in the situation in which they are.

His word is with authority, not like that of the Scribes, Mark 1.22, Matt. 7.28–9. His word is with power, just as his works of healing are δυνάμεις, mighty works. So it is that St. John speaks of him as 'the Word of God'; it is not merely that in his utterances he speaks God's Word, but rather that he himself in his own person *is* God's Word. Origen coined for him later the term αὐτοβασιλεία, which cannot be translated but only paraphrased: 'He-is-the-Kingdom'.[1] In his person is embodied all that the Kingdom and Reign and Kingly Rule of God means. This is implied in the phrase which occurs twice in Mark 'for my sake and the Gospel's'; in Mark 10.29 of leaving home and relatives and lands, and in 8.35 of the surrender of life itself. For Jesus *is* the Gospel.

The carrying through of his mission to the end, and the pressing home of the challenge of the real Kingdom of God—to the exclusion of all substitutes for the real thing, such as a correct observance of all the rules of the Law, or a nationalistic Kingdom of Israel—cost him his life: for the challenge was more than men dared to face. It absolutely demanded a 'Yes', or a 'No'; and their 'No' was his condemnation to be crucified as the Accursed One. When he had been vindicated by God

---

[1] Cf. Hebert, *The Throne of David*, p. 138 n.

himself in the resurrection, and the apostles were left to carry on the mission, what was the Apostolic Message?

Inevitably and necessarily, the Proclaimer now became the Proclaimed One.[1] The apostles proclaimed Jesus, that he was the Messiah and the Son of God. The Kingdom of God was what Jesus had proclaimed it to be. He had brought to men the personal challenge of the Kingdom: to the sick he had brought healing, to tax collectors and sinners and other sick souls the forgiveness of sins. The apostles themselves in the first passiontide and Easter had known what it meant to be raised from death to life, and to receive the fullness of forgiveness for their own sin. The same was now to be true for all. At Pentecost, we are told in Acts 2.38 that Peter's word was, 'Repent and be baptized every one of you in the name of Jesus the Messiah for the forgiveness of your sins: and you will receive the gift of the Holy Spirit.' Later, when Peter goes to visit the Roman centurion Cornelius, the same happens for Gentiles also; and Peter thus describes it in Acts 11.15 ff.: 'Hardly had I begun speaking, when the Holy Spirit came upon them, just as upon us at the beginning. Then I recalled what the Lord had said, "John baptized with water, but you will be baptized with the Holy Spirit". God gave them no less a gift than he gave us when we put our trust in the Lord Jesus Christ: then how could I possibly stand in God's way?' There is a true and essential continuity between the Gospel announced by the Proclaimer and that of the apostles who proclaimed him as the Messiah and the Son of God.

The outline of the Apostolic *Kerygma*—God's age-long purpose accomplished in Jesus, crucified, risen from the dead, exalted and glorified: therefore believe, repent, be baptized— is familiar to all from Dr. Dodd's book, *The Apostolic Preaching and its Development*. With regard to the *kerygma*-speeches in Acts 2–5, 10 and 13, while we can allow for some touching-up by Luke himself, we have substantially the same apostolic message in St. Paul's epistles, as Dodd showed in his book; and the fact

---

[1] This is Bultmann's phrase, and it is right. The rest of the paragraph is an endeavour to show what Bultmann missed.

remains that the phrasing of the *kerygma* in the early chapters of Acts does appear to be primitive, and pre-Pauline.

Broadly speaking, the Apostolic Message is given to us in the whole New Testament. It underlies the synoptic gospels. It is presented in a systematic form in Romans (the divine work of salvation, and justification by the Grace of God, apprehended by faith) in Ephesians (the theology of the Church) and Hebrews (the High-priesthood of Christ and his Sacrifice). Elsewhere various aspects of the Message receive fairly detailed treatment—the apostles' mission in 2 Cor. 2.15–6.10; the universal Lordship of Christ in Colossians; the meaning of Christian *koinonia* in Philippians; while in 1 Corinthians we have a whole series of pastoral and practical applications of Gospel principles. In James, we have powerful preaching in the Jewish–Christian tradition, showing close parallels with Matthew, especially the Sermon on the Mount. In St. John's gospel, we have a review of the mission of Jesus, showing the theology which actually underlies the earlier gospels. All this gives us the apostolic message, in the broad sense.

Finally, the essential continuity between the Gospel proclaimed by Jesus during his ministry and the apostolic message is emphasized in the texts which set out his commission to the apostles. First, there are the words of the commission in John 20.21–3, where the risen Lord says to them, 'As the Father sent me, so I send you.' He then breathed on them, saying, 'Receive the Holy Spirit. If you forgive any man's sins, they are forgiven; if you pronounce them unforgiven, unforgiven they remain.' These last words could apply not only to an excommunication, as in 1 Cor. 5.1–5, but also to the acceptance or postponement or refusal of applications for Baptism. In John 21.15–17 Peter, who had denied him three times, receives the threefold charge to feed and to tend the Lord's lambs and the Lord's sheep. So it is in St. Matthew's gospel, in which a main theme is that of discipleship to Jesus; in 28.16–20 Jesus on the mountain in Galilee meets with the eleven disciples—who are 'disciples' still though their training by him is now complete—and says to them: 'Full authority in heaven and on earth has been

The Apostolic Commission

committed to me. Go forth therefore and make all nations my disciples; baptize men everywhere in the name of the Father and of the Son and of the Holy Spirit, and teach them to observe all that I have commanded you. And be assured, I am with you always, to the end of time.' In Matthew 10 we have the mission of the Twelve during the ministry; but this chapter as a whole brings together a great number of sayings about the apostolic mission, some of which, such as vv. 17–20, manifestly apply to the period after the resurrection. They are sent out (vv. 7–8) with the words, 'As you go, proclaim the message, "The Kingdom of Heaven is upon you". Heal the sick, raise the dead, cleanse lepers, cast out devils. You received without cost: give without charge.' The comment to be made here is that the words 'Heal the sick' etc., are plainly an echo of his words about his own ministry in 11.5, 'The blind receive their sight, the lame walk, the lepers are clean, the deaf hear, the dead are raised to life, the poor are hearing the good news.' It is the same work; but the difference is that their authority is derived from his: as the old version has it in 10.8, 'Freely ye have received, freely give.'

In Matthew we have also the Charge to St. Peter, 16.17–19, and the parallel charge to the Twelve in 18.15–18, about church discipline. Here I wish to quote some words that I have lately written elsewhere,[1] summarizing Bornkamm's observation, that both these passages must be seen in the context in which our Evangelist inserts them:

'The Petrine text is inserted in a wholly Markan section, Matt. 16.13–28, which contains Peter's Confession—then the Petrine text—then the first passion-prophecy, Peter's objection, and the word to him "Get thee behind me, Satan", then the call to all the disciples to deny the self and carry the cross, and the word about the final Advent of the Son of man in glory "to render to each man according to his works", in-

[1] In my article on 'The Problem of the Gospel according to Matthew' in the *Scottish Journal of Theology*, Vol. 14, No. 4 (Dec. 1961). The reference to Prof. Bornkamm is to his essay in *The Background of the New Testament and its Eschatology*, ed. Davies and Daube, pp. 256–9.

cluding all who exercise the ministry of stewardship and have authority to forbid and permit. The later passage, 18.15–18, comes within the Fourth Discourse of 18.1–35, which contains the disciples' question to him, "Who is the greatest?", and his answer about humility, and receiving the little ones, and the terrible guilt of leading them into sin— then the passage about church discipline—then the duty of forgiving others, with the mighty parable of the man forgiven the debt of 10,000 talents whose forgiveness is cancelled when he will not forgive others. Such is the context of the teaching about Church discipline.'

It is clear that the Apostolic Commission includes not only the proclamation of their message, but also the ministry of the sacraments and the pastoral and disciplinary care of their converts. To be 'a witness to his resurrection' was the beginning of the responsibility of an apostle of Jesus; but it was not the whole, even though all the rest had to be seen in the light of his resurrection.

(iv) *The Ministry of the Apostles*

About St. Paul's ministry we know a very great deal; much from Acts about the early part of St. Peter's, and more if the first epistle is his; a little about that of St. James, and more if the epistle is his; and if in St. John's gospel the 'Beloved Disciple' really is John son of Zebedee—and it is hard to see who else he can be—then John 21 is proof that John the Apostle lived to a very great age, so that some people were thinking that he was being kept for the Lord's Advent. If so, it seems to follow that if the gospel was not written by him, it was written by one who had sat at his feet and wished to give to the Church Saint John's Gospel. But of the ministry of the other members of the Twelve, we know nothing. And that is perhaps a further reason for being sure that our Lord really did call the Twelve; it would be strange indeed if such a belief were to arise without any historical foundation about twelve disciples of whom the Church's tradition had nothing to relate, apart from three leaders—and Judas Iscariot.

The Ministry of the Apostles

It is clear from what we do know that the ministry of the apostles involved not only their testimony to the resurrection and their proclamation of the *kerygma*, but also the pastoral care of the baptized. I owe to Prof. Harald Riesenfeld of Uppsala the idea of the following scheme of the theological relation of their ministry to the glorified Lord.[1] It is based on the images of the Church as the Family or Household, the Temple, the Flock, and the Bride.

Christ is *the Master of the House* (Matt. 10.25). The Church is a Household or Family, which calls on God as 'Our Father'. In it the Apostles are stewards, holding the keys of stewardship, Matt. 16.19, and responsible for the management of the household and the provision of food, Luke 12.41 ff. The keys are, of course, the keys of the cupboards, as we might say, not the keys of the front door. Matt. 16.19 does not designate St. Peter as a door-keeper.

Christ is *the Head Corner-stone* which God has laid; the Stone rejected by the builders, but which no power of earth or of hell could prevent from going into its place, Mark 12.10–11 (quoting Psalm 118.22–3, as do Acts 4.11 and 1 Peter 2.6 ff.). There had also been a saying of Jesus about a 'Temple made without hands' which would replace Herod's temple, Mark 14.58, and John 2.19 where the evangelist's comment is that 'the temple he was speaking of was his body', that is, his body which was to rise from the dead and also his body the Church. In Eph. 2.19 ff. the Christians are said to be first 'fellow-citizens with God's people', then 'members of God's household', and then stones in God's temple, which is 'built on the foundation laid by the apostles and prophets' and of which 'Christ Jesus himself is the foundation-stone. In him the whole building is bonded together and grows into a holy temple in the Lord'. Already St. Paul had developed in 1 Cor. 3.10–17 the imagery of the Church as 'God's temple, where the Spirit of God dwells', v. 16; and 'there can be no other foundation than that which

[1] Cf. Prof. Riesenfeld's essay in *The Root of the Vine*, Essays in Biblical Theology by Anton Fridrichsen and others. Dacre Press (1953), esp. pp. 106–9.

is already laid: I mean, Jesus Christ himself'. Of this temple, as he says in v. 10, an apostle is a 'master-builder'; cf. Eph. 2.20, quoted above.

Christ is *the Good Shepherd*, John 10.11–16, of a universal Flock into which the 'other sheep' of all nations are to come; and as there is One Shepherd, so there is to be One Flock. In the Church the Apostles are under-shepherds charged to 'feed' the flock. This image comes again in 1 Peter 5.4, which is addressed to the Elders or Presbyters of the Church.

Christ is *the Bridegroom* and the Church his Bride, Eph. 5.25–32. So in Matt. 22.1 he is the King's Son at his Wedding-feast, and the same in 25.1 ff., the parable of the Ten Virgins. In terms of this image, the apostle's work is to introduce the Bride to the Bridegroom, 2 Cor. 11.2.

Here are four images with one common structure, showing that the apostolic functions are permanently necessary in the Church; for each of the instances we have given is directly connected with an Apostle, either Peter or Paul. Others also participate in them. At Corinth, if Paul laid the foundation, others continued the work: if Paul planted, Apollos watered, 1 Cor. 3.6, 10. Colossae was founded seemingly by Epaphras, Col. 1.6–7; Antioch, much earlier by unnamed Christians after the Stephen-persecution, Acts 11.19–21, and it was only later that an apostolic man arrived from Jerusalem, vv. 22 f. We have no information, similarly, about the founding of the Church of Rome. But it is in regard to the function of 'shepherding' that the evidence is clearest. In 1 Peter 5.1–4 the Elders or Presbyters are charged by St. Peter—if the epistle is his—with the shepherding of the flock, and that this is to be done not as a matter of mere duty, nor for the sake of any stipend, nor despotically, but devotedly, out of love; for Christ himself is the Chief Shepherd. It is interesting that St. Peter calls himself also an Elder, as being an older man and a witness of the Lord's passion, and in v. 5 goes on to speak to the 'younger men'. The New Testament speaks regularly of 'functions' rather than 'offices', even though without doubt both Apostleship and Presbytership were offices.

The Ministry of the Apostles

The word *episkopos*, however, does not anywhere in the New Testament denote an office, or mean what we mean by 'a bishop'. It was one of the merits of *The Apostolic Ministry* that this was made very clear: *episkopos* means any person, most often a presbyter, who exercises *episkopē* or pastoral charge. In Acts 20.17 St. Paul summons the presbyters of Ephesus to Miletus, and in v. 28 addresses them as *episkopoi*; in Phil. 1.1 he speaks of the *episkopoi* and deacons at Philippi. The *episkopoi* were presbyters after the pattern of a Jewish synagogue. The same is true of the Pastoral Epistles, where 1 Tim. 5.17 shows they did not all exercise *episkopē*: 'Elders who do well as leaders should be reckoned worthy of a double stipend, especially those who labour at preaching and teaching.' This seems to be the point of 3.1, where it is said that to desire to exercise *episkopē* is honourable; for these words were not written to commend clerical ambition.[1] There were also Deacons at Philippi, as also in the Pastoral Epistles; these seem to be younger church officers, capable of promotion later, as 1 Tim. 3.13 suggests; the word *presbyteroi* in 5.1–2 can still be used simply of 'older men' as contrasted with young men. There seem also to have been 'deaconesses' holding a regular church office, like Phoebe in Romans 16.1; and it would be possible to translate *gynaikas* in 1 Tim. 3.11 as 'women deacons', though the more probable translation is 'their wives'. There were also, of course, prophets in the apostolic church, but theirs was a personal gift and they were not church officers.

The word *episkopos* is used once of Christ himself, 'the Shepherd and Bishop of your souls', 1 Peter 2.25, just as the words 'Apostle' and 'Highpriest' are his titles in Hebrews 3.1. The emphasis of the New Testament is consistent here. There was indeed a church order; but Matt. 23.8–12 is typical and not exceptional in forbidding not only the coveting but even the use of titles such as 'rabbi' or 'father' or 'teacher'. 'You have one Teacher, the Messiah. The greatest among you must be your servant. For whoever exalts himself

[1] This unfortunate suggestion is made in the NEB, the meaning of *episkopē* being missed.

will be humbled, and whoever humbles himself will be exalted.'

It appears, then, that the Preface to the English Ordinal is scarcely correct when it affirms that, 'It is evident unto all men, diligently reading Holy Scripture and ancient Authors, that from the Apostles' time there have been these Orders of Ministers in Christ's Church: Bishops, Priests and Deacons.' This sentence might read in modern English: 'All biblical and patristic scholars are agreed that from the time of the Apostles the Orders of Bishops, Priests and Deacons have existed in the Christian Church.' But in the New Testament *episkopos*, as we have seen, nowhere denotes an Order of the Ministry, the word 'priest' is nowhere the title of a Christian Minister, and the Deacons of that day were not half-fledged Presbyters. On the face of it, scholarship does not support this famous sentence from the Preface to the Ordinal.

Yet that sentence is not to be thus summarily dismissed. It does not claim that our Lord instituted the Ministry just as we have it now; it only traces that Ministry back to the Apostles' time. In the next chapter we shall consider whether scholarship allows us to find a real continuity of the episcopal Ministry of the Church with the Apostolic Commission, which, as we have seen in this chapter, has a true continuity with the Gospel-message which our Lord proclaimed.

CHAPTER IV

From Apostolate to Episcopate

★

We come now to a difficult and controversial part of our subject, where those of one side are tempted to argue the case for episcopacy, and those of the other side to seek to refute any such argument. Yet we are aware in these days that it is not well that divided Christians should bite and devour one another; and so it must be in this particular discussion. It is possible in historical inquiries to seek the truth without distorting the facts. In regard to the interpretation of the facts, both parties can agree that there are two sides to the matter; on the one side, that in the second century there was the sense of a divinely-given authority in the Christian Ministry, and on the other, the sense of the Holy Spirit animating the whole body of the faithful. Correspondingly, there are the two questions: Was the authority of the apostles passed on in some real measure to the episcopate? Or did the monarchical bishop begin by being the chairman or president of each local presbyterate? There are some points here which can be historically established; but at other points the evidence is seriously defective, and this is the 'tunnel-period'.

It is not likely that we who live under Episcopacy will be able to demonstrate the truth of our view of the second-century developments, to the satisfaction of those who do not know Episcopacy from within. Yet, as has been said on pp. 31–2, it is right for us to use our experience of life in the Church today to help us in interpreting the evidence of the Church's life in the

53

past.[1] Thus, we have argued in the previous chapter that our Lord really did choose the Twelve, and that the Twelve were recognized in our very earliest sources to be distinct from the Five hundred, because we held that the evidence was adequate. At the same time our dialogue with those of the other side compels us to beware lest in our exposition we insinuate anything like 'clerical pretensions', and forget the attitude enjoined on the holders of church authority in 1 Peter 5.1-4.

(i) *Canon of Scripture, Creed and Episcopate*

It is a point that was not clear, at least to my own mind, when *The Apostolic Ministry* was written, but is generally understood now, that in the later second century, before and after 180, three things became definitely fixed: the chief books of our New Testament were accepted as canonical Scripture, side by side with the Old Testament: the Apostles' Creed was taking a definite shape: and there were Bishops presiding everywhere in all the churches.

(a) The New Testament Canon did not indeed reach its final form till the fourth century; in some parts of the Church two important books, Hebrews and the Apocalypse, were still 'disputed', and some of the shorter epistles. But the rejection of the Old Testament by Marcion, and his bowdlerized version of the Christian books, forced the Church to put out its own canon of Scripture, consisting of the Old Testament, and the New Testament as the authentic apostolic testimony. To Irenaeus it is clear that there are four gospels only, just as there are

---

[1] 'If a man, on the authority of that body in which he has found the *Una Sancta*, has accepted a doctrine, institution or practice as belonging to its essence, a challenge to the latter on critico-historical grounds can be sufficiently met by a demonstration that its originality in some sense is not impossible. If he has never accepted it, there will be nothing to determine him in its favour, and nothing short of conclusive historical demonstration, of a kind rarely provided in these questions, will serve to convince him. An historical defence of what one has is very different from a historical argument for what one has not.'—Benedict Green, C. R. in his article 'The Apostolic Succession and the Anglican Appeal to History', in the *Church Quarterly Review*, July–Sept. 1962, pp. 295–6.

four winds and four cherubim;[1] but it is plain that Justin
Martyr had been unable to appeal to canonical gospels in this
way.[2] There had indeed been an earlier collection of Pauline
epistles, made probably before the end of the first century;[3] but
it probably did not include 2 Corinthians, since this seems to
have been unknown to Clement of Rome, Ignatius and Polycarp,[4] nor the Pastoral Epistles. Now, these are included, with
Acts, 1 John and 1 Peter.

(b) The Apostles' Creed did not reach its final form till the
sixth century. But already in the later second century the 'Old
Roman Creed' had taken shape.[5] The central point here is
what we call the Apostolic Kerygma; in Hippolytus's baptismal
rite this appears in an interrogative form, addressed to the
candidates for baptism at the moment when the water is poured
over them, and the wording is to a large extent the same as in
our Apostles' Creed. There is first the confession of faith in God
as the creator; it was necessary for converts from paganism to
affirm this, whereas in the first century converts from Judaism
would not have needed to do so. Then comes the confession of
faith, as Hippolytus has it, in 'Christ Jesus the Son of God, born
of the Holy Spirit and the Virgin Mary, who was crucified in
the days of Pontius Pilate, and died and was buried, and rose
on the third day living from the dead, and ascended into
heaven, and sat down at the right hand of the Father, and will
come to judge the living and the dead.' Then comes the confession of faith in 'the Holy Spirit in the Holy Church' and the
resurrection of the flesh;[6] this last was necessary for converts
from paganism. There are parallels to Hippolytus's phrases in
Tertullian and Irenaeus.

[1] Irenaeus, *adv. Haereses*, II, xi, 8.
[2] John Knox, *The Early Church and the Coming Great Church*, Epworth Press
(1957), p. 115.
[3] e.g. E. J. Goodspeed, *New Solutions of New Testament Problems*, Chicago
(1927).
[4] G. Bornkamm in *New Testament Studies*, April 1962, pp. 263–4.
[5] See J. N. D. Kelly, *Early Christian Creeds*, Oxford (1950).
[6] Hippolytus, *The Apostolic Tradition* (ed. Dix), Ch. XXI, pp. 36–7, and
pp. lx ff.

From Apostolate to Episcopate

(c) The third point is the Episcopate, which certainly existed everywhere in the Church well before the end of the second century. Indeed, at the beginning of the century, St. Ignatius of Antioch writes his seven letters to the churches of Asia Minor and of Rome, whither he is going to be martyred, and in every case, with the exception of Rome, he writes to the local bishop. One of these is Polycarp of Smyrna, who became a martyr in 155 at the age of eighty-eight. It looks as if in Rome and Alexandria also, the older order of government by presbyters survived longest: yet at Rome St. Clement writes his epistle to Corinth on behalf of the Roman Church.

We have, however, to notice that a distinction already existed then, which may be illustrated by our distinction between a bishop and an archbishop. The local bishop was then the president of a small Christian community in a city; and the great well-established churches in the capital cities would naturally exercise authority over the small churches in the area —such churches as Antioch in Syria (Ignatius in his letter to the Romans, ch. 2, calls himself the 'bishop of Syria') or Ephesus in Asia Minor, or Rome in Italy and seemingly Greece also, as Clement's letter to Corinth shows. This authority was quite undefined, but it would in the nature of the case be real.

All these three things, Canon and Creed and Episcopate, look back to the Apostles and their testimony as setting the norm and standard for the Church's faith and life. The New Testament was the expression of the Apostolic Testimony; its books carried the names of apostles or disciples of apostles such as Mark or Luke, and it perpetuated the witness of the apostles to the resurrection of the Lord. The Creed was basically the original apostolic preaching. And the Episcopate, especially that of the great churches founded by apostles, witnessed to the authentic tradition of the Christian Faith which was preserved there. The great importance of this threefold appeal to the apostles was that the Church was in the midst of its life-and-death struggle with the Gnosticism which sought to interpret the Faith in terms of the Greek conception of salvation by right knowledge, and which denied the redemption of the body.

Scripture, Creed, Episcopate

Gnosticism was a religion for the superior person, and it exercized a fatal attraction on the intellectuals of the age. But it was vital for the Church to hold fast to the principle of the redemption of the whole of man's life and not merely of his intellectual and religious aspirations: therefore it must hold fast to the Incarnation of the Son of God as true man, his real death and his real resurrection. All this stood in line with its inheritance from old Israel, and the Old Testament Scriptures: therefore even Marcion, the most Christian of Gnostics, must be rejected because he refused to recognize the Old Testament. We shall say on pp. 65–6 that this conflict with Gnosticism can have been the thing which made it necessary that each local church should have its Bishop.

Hence the Apostolic Succession in the second century means in the first place the succession of the bishops in their sees, like the succession of the Roman Popes or of the Archbishops of Canterbury, of which Archbishop Ramsey is the hundredth occupant. Lists of bishops of the great sees were made out, especially by Hegesippus, because the key-point was the witness of those sees to the apostolic faith. The other meaning of Apostolic Succession, through the laying on of hands, received for the time being little emphasis, though, as we shall see, Hippolytus's rite for the consecration of a bishop implies that there had been a continuous succession-by-ordination.

Let us note also that the objection to the whole idea of succession, that a *shaliach* could not pass on to another the authority committed to him,[1] holds good only in the case of a Jewish *shaliach*. But an Apostle was a *shaliach* of Jesus, and this made all the difference. The Apostle was entrusted with the Lord's Gospel-message, and with the care of the churches: these were essential functions in the Church's mission, and therefore must be handed on. Already in New Testament times there had been apostolic delegates, like Timothy and Titus acting under St. Paul.

[1] pp. 22–3 above.

From Apostolate to Episcopate

(ii) *Apostolic Delegates and Local Bishops*

St. Paul had made use of Timothy and Titus from quite early times in the oversight of the Church at Corinth.[1] In the Pastoral Epistles, Timothy and Titus are apostolic delegates, having charge of an area, Asia Minor or Crete. If these epistles were written by St. Paul or under his direction, this point is evident. But for our present inquiry, these epistles are equally helpful if they are not Pauline. In this case, since they can hardly be later than 85 or 90 (for they do not reflect the church order of the Epistles of St. Ignatius), we must reckon that Timothy and Titus would be well-known names in the Church of that date, for Timothy would seem to have been not much over twenty in A.D. 50, when according to Acts 16.1 St. Paul took him as his assistant, and he could well have lived till A.D. 90. These men, in the Pastoral Epistles, have oversight over a number of local churches, and are responsible for looking after presbyters, deacons, and widows, for seeing that sound doctrine is taught everywhere, and that church discipline is well maintained.

Other instances of oversight over groups of local churches appear in the letters to the Seven Churches in Rev. 1–3; and again in 3 John, which is addressed by John the Elder (who is presumably the author of the Fourth Gospel) to Gaius, and calls for an exercise of church discipline in the case of Diotrephes, who appears to be an ambitious and self-willed man who wants to be recognized as 'bishop' of a local church; but the right man for the post is Demetrius (3 John 9–12).

Then there is the oversight of Corinth by Clement of Rome; but it is not surprising that I Clement 42–4 should be a controverted passage, since ch. 44 contains one disputed reading (*epinomin* or *epimonēn*), and one word (*ellogimoi*) whose meaning is disputed, and ambiguous pronouns where he says that the Apostles arranged 'that if *they* should fall asleep other *ellogimoi* men should succeed to *their* ministry'. Do the pronouns refer to

---

[1] Timothy, 1 Cor. 4.17; 16.10; Titus, 2 Cor. 2.13; 7.6, 13–14; 8.6, 16, 23; 12.18.

the Corinthian presbyters and the problem of the succession there, or to successors of the Apostles? If the latter, is it being claimed that the Roman church holds an apostolic authority? Such a problem of interpretation cannot be discussed here. In view of our own argument in this book, it is interesting that the discussion begins in ch. 42 with the Gospel proclaimed by the Lord, and received by the Apostles from him.

By what stages did the monarchical bishop emerge as the president of each local church? We are unable to say; for this is the actual 'tunnel period', where the evidence is defective. We find monarchical bishops in Ignatius, but nothing about the manner of their appointment or their consecration to the episcopate; we get nothing of this sort till Hippolytus. Thus, while in the New Testament there is good evidence for apostolic delegates with authority over groups of local churches, and we know that in the course of the second century bishops emerged as presidents of local churches, what we do not know is just how these two different functions came together in the one office of 'bishop'.

Was it the case that the episcopate emerged 'from below', in the sense that the Chairman of the Board of Presbyters became *the* 'bishop', *the* holder of *episkopē*? This could well happen, in view of the important consideration of the presidency of the weekly Eucharist, on the occasion when the local Church *assembled, together, as the People of God,* to make the memorial of the Lord's death which he had commanded. It is worth while to study the occurrence of these three words or phrases, for which the Greek is *synerchesthai, epi to auto,* and *en ecclesia* respectively, in 1 Cor. 11.17–34; the first of them occurs in this passage five times, and the other two once each. The Presbyter who regularly presided at this solemn assembly of the Church could soon come to be regarded as the President of the local community. Or was it that the office of apostolic delegates came to impose itself as 'from above', on each local community? It is here that the evidence fails. What we know is that by the time of Hippolytus the local bishop is consecrated by bishops from other churches, while the ordination to the board of presbyters is by the local bishop, with the other presbyters all joining in the laying on of hands.

Before we go on to this, it is important to notice how clearly the apostles in the New Testament are related to the Church-community as a whole. In Acts 1, Peter calls the whole community together, to see the place of the Twelfth Apostle filled: in Acts 2.1, they are all 'together' (*epi to auto*) when the Holy Spirit comes at Pentecost, and this phrase comes again in 2.47. In Acts 6, 1–6 the election of 'the Seven' is by the whole community, just as in Hippolytus the election of the local bishop is by the whole community (Ap. Trad. ii, 1–2). Paul and Barnabas, after the missionary journey to Cyprus and Galatia, call together the *ecclesia* at Antioch, Acts 14.27, to tell them how God has opened a door of faith to the Gentiles. The Jerusalem Council, Acts 15, consists of apostles and presbyters. When Paul returns for his last visit to Jerusalem, to present the collection from the Gentile churches, he meets with James, and all the presbyters are present, Acts 21.18. The epistles of St. Paul are to be read to the whole community, Col. 4.16, and the same is implied at the end of 1 Cor. and 2 Cor., when he speaks of the Kiss of Peace which is exchanged among them all: in 1 Thess. 5.27 he gives a solemn command that the epistle is to be read to all. In 1 Cor. 5, he pictures the Church Meeting at Corinth to pronounce excommunication on the men guilty of incest, he himself being 'absent in body but present in spirit' (5.3–5). In 2 Cor. 2.6 he alludes to a similar Meeting which has dealt with the ringleader who has been causing trouble at Corinth. In the Philippian epistle (esp. 1.3–11) we have the matchless picture of the unity of the Christian community in Christ, uniting them with one another and with him in his absence from them.

Such evidence as we have of the period during which the monarchical episcopate was emerging suggests that the relation between the holders of authority and those subject to them remained equally close. We shall be brought back to this point again in the next chapter.[1]

[1] pp. 71–2 below.

(iii) *Ordination Rites in Hippolytus*

We have said that 'apostolic succession' regularly means in the second century the succession of the bishops in a particular See. But there must have been some form of ordination, just as in a Jewish synagogue the *zeqenim* or presbyter-elders were ordained by the *semikah* or laying-on of hands by those already ordained.[1] So in the Pastoral Epistles Timothy is charged not to neglect the gift (*charisma*) given by 'the laying-on of hands of the Presbytery' (1 Tim. 4.14) and of St. Paul's own hands (2 Tim. 1.6)—texts which may perhaps refer to two different occasions.

(a) *The Consecration of a Bishop* in Ap. Trad., ii–vii is performed by bishops, who must belong of course to other churches, after the candidate has been duly elected by all the people. The prayer said over him by the presiding bishop speaks first of God's ordinances given to his Church from Abraham onwards; and then he prays God to impart to him 'the princely Spirit which thou didst deliver to thy Beloved Servant Jesus Christ, which he bestowed on thy holy apostles who established in every place the Church which hallows thee. . . .' Then the functions of the bishop-elect are specified: 'To shepherd thy holy flock'; 'To serve as thy high-priest, blamelessly ministering by night and day, ceaselessly to propitiate thy countenance and to offer to thee the gifts of thy holy Church' (in the Eucharist): 'By the high-priestly Spirit to have authority to forgive sins according to thy command, to give lots (i.e. ordain) according to thy bidding, to loose every bond (i.e. exorcise and heal) according to the authority which thou didst give to the apostles'; 'To please thee in meekness and a pure heart, offering to thee the savour of sweetness.' The eucharistic celebration follows.

On this there are three comments to be made. First: here we have plainly the conception of Apostolic Succession by Ordination. The Holy Spirit who is invoked upon the bishop-elect is the Spirit bestowed by the Lord Jesus Christ on his apostles. We shall come in a moment to the prayer at the ordination of

[1] *The Apostolic Ministry*, pp. 217, 233–4 (Dix).

presbyters, which is different. Here the petition is, not for a *transmission* of a divine gift from the bishop who consecrates to him who is consecrated, but for *a fresh creative divine act*, bestowing the Spirit on each new bishop. So Gregory Dix writes in a striking passage on p. 200 of *The Apostolic Ministry*.

But it is not necessary to follow him in the further claim that each episcopal consecration was and is an actual addition to the College of Apostles, so that a Bishop *is* an Apostle. For this, surely, is not the case. The Apostles of Jesus stand by themselves; they belong to the time of the Church's foundation; they are 'witnesses of the Resurrection'; and their teaching, embodied in the New Testament, is normative for the Church. In this sense, no successors of the apostles could stand on a level with them. At the same time, they must have successors in the continuing proclamation of the Word, the ministry of the Sacraments and the care of all the churches; and the bishops of the Church are their successors.[1]

The third comment must be that there are phrases in Hippolytus's rite, phrases due no doubt to Hippolytus himself, that give us pause. Coming not long after Marcion who had rejected the Old Testament, and perhaps in reaction against him, he makes what appears to be an improper use of the Old Testament at two points. He calls the bishop a 'highpriest' by analogy with the Old Testament hierarchical system, as Tertullian had done a little earlier; this is not in itself improper,[2] but it is a fault that he does not in any way relate it to the Highpriesthood of Christ. The other point concerns the word 'propitiation', of which we shall have more to say later;[3] when he says that the bishop is 'to propitiate thy countenance and to offer the gifts of thy holy

[1] The second-century writers, such as Irenaeus (*c.* Haer. III, iii. 3) and Tertullian (*de Praescriptions*, 32), state clearly that the Apostles were founders of churches, and were not to be reckoned as 'bishops' of those churches. With Cyprian in the third century a different view begins to come in, that apostolate and episcopate are shared jointly by all holders of these offices, and this view became fairly general in the West, but never in the East.— Dvornik in *The Idea of Apostolicity in Byzantium*, Harvard (1958), pp. 34–5, 39–48.

[2] Cf. pp. 71–4 below.

[3] pp. 106–7, and other references in Ch. VII below.

Church' in the eucharistic action, he is using the word 'propitiate' in the sense in which it occurs in some places in the Old
Testament, without regard to the New Testament interpretation of the word in 1 John 4.10, where St. John speaks of Jesus
Christ as him 'whom God sent, to be the propitiation for our
sins', or as N.E.B. translates, 'as the remedy for the defilement
of our sins'.

(b) *The ordination of a Presbyter*[1] begins, as C. H. Turner has
perhaps proved, with the same words as those used for a bishop,
about the Old Testament ordinances and the Spirit bestowed by
Jesus on his apostles. Then, God is prayed, on behalf of the new
Presbyter, to 'look upon this thy servant and fill him with the
Spirit of grace and counsel, to share in the presbyterate and
govern the people with a pure heart' ('and teach'—but, says
Dix, the wording of this clause cannot be restored); 'as thou
didst look upon the People of thy choice, and command Moses
to choose presbyters, whom thou didst fill with the Spirit which
thou hadst given to thy servant, so now, O Lord, grant (that it
be so unto us), preserving uninterrupted among us the Spirit of
thy grace, and grant that believing in thee they may serve thee
in singleness of heart.'

In the ordination of presbyters the existing presbyters join
with the bishop in the laying on of hands, as they do in Roman
Catholic and Anglican presbyteral ordinations today. In Hippolytus they are acting as members of the presbyteral college
accepting a new member, as presumably they had done in the
apostolic age in such a church as Corinth, and as Jewish synagogue elders had been accustomed to do. Gregory Dix suggests
that the prayer in Hippolytus 'might so far as its substance is
concerned go back to the earliest Jewish–Christian synagogues,
and even to Jewish practice', and the mention of Moses' ordination of his seventy Elders supports this.[2]

We must notice that nothing is said in this presbyteral ordina-
tion-rite of any liturgical functions of the presbyter; there is
nothing for instance about any participation of presbyters in the

---

[1] *The Apostolic Ministry*, pp. 216 ff. Hippolytus, Ch. VIII.
[2] *The Apostolic Ministry*, p. 218. Cf. also pp. 144–5 below.

baptismal or eucharistic rites. He is to 'govern', as a member of the board which is responsible for church administration, and to teach. If the bishop of each church had a chief part in the framing of church policy, as he must have had, he would have to get the consent of the presbyteral council to all that he did.

(c) About *the making of a Deacon*[1] little need be said here. His specified functions, in striking contrast with those of the presbyters, are first of all liturgical: he is to 'minister to thy Church, to bring up in holiness to thy holiness that which is offered to thee by thy appointed high-priests to the glory of thy Name'— that is to say, at the Eucharist he will bring to the eucharistic president the bread and wine and other gifts which the people offer. Elsewhere in the *Apostolic Tradition*, in Chapter XXX, it is said that the deacons are to wait upon the bishop, and report the names of sick people to him that he may visit them. The deacon is ordained by the bishop only; the presbyters have no share in this.

The Seven who are ordained in Acts 6 were not Deacons.[2] St. Luke says that they were ordained to 'serve tables' and see that the 'hellenistic' widows did not go short of charitable relief; the functions of deacons in St. Luke's own day would have been similar. Yet Stephen and Philip are not said to do this at all, but to engage in quite other activities. It would seem that the accounts of St. Stephen's work in the hellenistic synagogue and his consequent martyrdom, and of Philip's subsequent evangelistic work, are authentic enough, and so is the situation described at Jerusalem where the widows needed charitable relief; but that St. Luke, who has no occasion elsewhere to allude in his narrative to the ministry of the Diaconate, has chosen to link this up with the ordination of the Seven.

In the Pastoral Epistles nothing is said of the functions of deacons; but they are distinguished from presbyters, and 1 Tim. 3.13 suggests that they are young. In Hippolytus their functions are liturgical and charitable, but they do not appear to engage, like Stephen and Philip, in active evangelistic work. Even the

[1] ibid., p. 225. Hippolytus, Ch. IX.
[2] *The Apostolic Ministry*, p. 138 f. (Farrer).

reading of the Gospel in the liturgy, which later became the deacon's special privilege, is not mentioned in Hippolytus.

It is time now to gather up the threads of our discussion in this chapter. First, we have the fixing of the Canon and Creed and Episcopate, at about the same time. All three point directly back to the Apostolic Testimony as basic for the Church's teaching and life. The inference is that the Episcopate can claim by right the same degree of authority as the other two.

We have also fixed the meaning of the 'tunnel-period' where the evidence is defective. It comes at the point where those who have authority over groups of local churches, the successors of the earlier apostolic delegates share the episcopal office with the chairmen of the councils of presbyters in the local churches. We do not know the process by which this happened; but we know that by the end of the second century it had happened, and there were everywhere bishops both of the great churches, having real authority over local churches in their area, and bishops in each local church, not as holders of the apostolic office itself, but as successors of the apostles.

But—and this is the really important point—this is not a mere matter of church organization. The guardianship of the Gospel-message was in the middle first century in the hands of the apostles, together with the 'care of all the churches'. In the second century, the bishops of the great churches were responsible for leadership in the life-and-death struggle with Gnosticism, which denied the redemption of the body, and rejected the true manhood of the incarnate Lord, regarding salvation primarily as a way of knowledge for the intellectual, and taking no interest in the common life and work of ordinary people. Thus the bishops of the great churches inherited the responsibility of the Apostolic Delegates for the guarding of the truth of the Gospel, as the Pastoral Epistles and the Johannine Epistles show. But the head of the small local church shared the same responsibility in his limited sphere; for then, as now, perils which threatened the whole Church would be real perils in each city and town. If, then, the office of Bishop was directly associated with the guardianship of the truth of the Gospel according to the Apostolic Testimony, the head of each local church needed to be a Bishop.

(iv) *Bishops and Presbyters in the Fourth and Fifth centuries*

In the fourth century a great change took place, which belongs not to what Gregory Dix calls the 'constitutional' history of the Episcopate, but to its 'administrative' history.[1] He reminds us how historians distinguish 'between "constitutional history" proper, which deals with the structure of institutions and the theory of their functions, and "administrative history" which deals with their day-to-day practical working and their inherence in the concrete historical situation of any given period'. He illustrates this from the changes in the actual work of a bishop in England, from the first bishops who were missionary monks, through the dark ages and the middle ages down to the present day. It could equally be illustrated from the history of the English monarchy. While constitutional forms remain relatively permanent, the actual functioning of an office in ecclesiastical and national affairs can become very different indeed.

Such a change happened in the fourth century in the Church to the offices of Bishop and Presbyter, though it was already beginning in the third. During the pre-Nicene period the bishop was the president of the local church, celebrating the Eucharist every Sunday with his people. In small churches he had perhaps only one deacon, and his council of presbyters. In the great church at Rome there were already forty-five presbyters in the middle of the third century and seven deacons, and already the presbyters must have begun to have charge of congregations in different parts of the great city. With the Peace of the Church in the fourth century there was an enormous increase in the numbers of Christians everywhere; the bishop, who hitherto had ruled the local church with his council of presbyters, now found it necessary to be away quite often attending councils of bishops,

---

[1] *The Apostolic Ministry*, pp. 187 ff., 291, 295.

whether ecumenical or provincial, and it was there and not in the local councils of presbyters that decisions of policy were made. Meanwhile the presbyter had become, with the increase of numbers, the rector of a city parish, fully occupied there; and the council of presbyters dropped more and more into the background.

The important thing, for the ordinary Christian, was the presidency of the Eucharist. Hitherto he had received the sacrament Sunday by Sunday at the hands of the bishop, who was the normal celebrant of the Liturgy. Now the presbyter became the normal liturgical celebrant, as he has continued to be till today. One result for the Church was that the check upon episcopal autocracy which had previously existed had now largely disappeared.[1] Previously, the presbyters had a positive right to be consulted on all the affairs of the Church. Now they had become a number of individual deputies of the bishop, with authority to perform a limited number of functions in a particular district.

Hence, by the end of the fourth century, it was possible for Jerome to ask, 'What does a bishop do that a presbyter cannot do except to ordain?' and to argue that the offices of bishop and presbyter were really and essentially one, having only this one difference.[2] For while the 'constitutional' structure of Church Order remained unchanged, its administrative functioning had deeply altered. The offices of Bishop and Presbyter came within one century to take the general shape which they have retained ever since.

It is important to have this change in mind when we are studying the origins of Episcopacy, and seeking to learn what its real nature is, particularly when we are concerned above all with the relation of the episcopal office to the Christian Gospel.

(v) *Valid Orders*

Throughout the patristic period there had been no formu-

---

[1] *The Apostolic Ministry*, p. 282 (Dix); cf. p. 64 above.
[2] ibid., pp. 307–49, Dr Jalland's essay on 'The Parity of Ministers'.

lated doctrine of Holy Orders. In Hippolytus's rite for the consecration of a bishop it is implied that there has been an unbroken succession of ordinations from the apostles onwards; and this was generally understood. In St. Cyprian's writings, the Christian Ministry is seen in close connection with the unity of the Church-community within which its functions are exercised. But with St. Augustine a view emerged which envisaged the real validity of orders outside the Church-community; and strangely enough, this theory arose out of an effort to restore church unity where it had been broken. The Donatists, who were specially strong in North Africa, were rigorists; like the Novatians of St. Cyprian's day, they wanted to have 'a Church of the Saints', and held that the Catholic view of the Church as humanly imperfect involved disloyalty to the Gospel. In the following centuries, a doctrine of valid orders based on St. Augustine's reply to the Donatists became the accepted view in the western Church, and this was the view that was vigorously reasserted in the Church of England by the Tractarians.

In the middle of the third century, St. Cyprian expressed the view of church order which the Eastern Churches have always retained. A typical passage is that of *Ep.* lxix, 5, where he begins, as he regularly does, with the Unity of the Church:

' "There is one Flock and one Shepherd." If there is one Flock, how can anyone be reckoned as part of the Flock who does not belong to it? Or how can anyone be held to be a pastor, if, while there remains the true Pastor, and while men hold office by successive ordinations, he himself stands in succession to no one, and thus, making a new beginning with himself, is in fact an interloper and a profane person?'[1]

Here there is indeed an emphasis on the succession, and a rigid view of it; but all is set within the context only of the believing and worshipping community, and the thought is that sacraments are real and valid only where there is the Church's shared faith and worship.

[1] I owe this quotation and the next one to H. R. T. Brandreth, *Episcopi Vagantes and the Anglican Church*, S.P.C.K., 2nd ed. (1961), pp. 8, 9. The translations are my own.

Valid Orders

But St. Augustine, inspired with the laudable motive of drawing the Donatists back into the unity of the Church, starts from the accepted belief that baptism is real and valid baptism by whoever it is administered; for there were many who had been baptized in emergency, when death was or seemed to be near, and this could be done by any Christian, clerical or lay. So then he tells the Donatists that as their baptisms are valid, so equally are their ordinations; let them return into the unity of the Great Church, and then with the return into unity their whole church life will be regularized and all will fall into place. He writes in the course of his disputation with a Donatist leader (*contra Epistolam Parmeniani*):

'There is no reason why one whose own baptism remains real and valid should lose the right to baptize others. For the two are both sacraments, and both involve that in the one way or in the other a person is consecrated, either when he is baptized or when he is ordained: hence in the Catholic Church neither of the two rites can be repeated. For when men come in from that party [Donatism] for the sake of peace, and the error of their schism is corrected and they are received, if it seems needful that they should continue to exercise the same office which they have been exercising they are not ordained again. Their ordination remains as valid (*integra*) as their baptism. The fault lay in their separation by schism, which has now been corrected and set right in the unity of peace, and not in the sacramental rites themselves, which are everywhere the same.'

Thus St. Augustine recognized the validity of Donatist ordinations, for they had retained the succession. Their ordinations were valid, as their baptisms were valid; all that was needed was their return into unity, and then such orders would acquire legitimacy and regularity.

Gregory Dix says of St. Augustine in *The Apostolic Ministry*, pp. 285–6:

'His is the pioneer work which is the basis of the whole later Western theology of orders, with its concept of the dependence of 'validity' and 'invalidity' solely upon the 'pedigree' (so to speak) of the ordainer. Thus we reach a conclusion which not only Cyprian but the whole pre-Nicene Church might have found rather startling, that it is possible by a series of historical accidents to have 'valid' orders outside the Church, combined with completely heretical views on most subjects, including the sacrament of orders itself. . . . This Augustine did not foresee, and might have repudiated had it ever been brought to his attention. But it followed inevitably from his position. . . . Many theologians would perhaps admit upon consideration that western Christendom today might have found its present difficulties easier of solution if its traditional theology *de ordine* had not been elaborated in such isolation from its theology *de ecclesia*. It is worth remembering that it was the urgent desire to end a schism which began this one-sided development.'

So this theory of Orders led the way to a conception of the Christian Ministry in which Episcopate and Priesthood could be seen as the possession of an individual, conferring on him personal gifts and privileges, rather than as being primarily the exercise of functions within the believing and worshipping community. It is not that the notion of Valid Orders is wrong in itself, for 'valid orders' are 'real orders'; it is that it becomes fatally one-sided, when the Office of the ordained minister is taken apart from his relation to the Church.

The Augustinian theory of Orders began as an expedient to end a schism. Much later, after other schisms had taken place, it could produce the quite extraordinary phenomenon of *episcopi vagantes*—bishops validly consecrated so far as the 'pedigree' of their consecrators went, but having no flocks at all to tend. It is plain that the Apostolic Succession which the Anglican Ordinal intended to assert does not demand any such one-sided theory of Orders as this.

CHAPTER V

From Middle Ages to Reformation

★

(i) *Authority in the Middle Ages*

In a remarkable study entitled 'The Historical Development of Authority in the Church: Points for Christian Reflection',[1] Père Yves Congar, O.P. starts with the Gospel, because without the Gospel the history of the Church is not intelligible. Running through his exposition is the relation of Church Authority or Hierarchy to the common life of the Church-community. I propose to begin this chapter with a résumé of what he has written, with frequent quotations, making it my aim to retain with entire faithfulness the balance of his argument.

'Hierarchy', he says, is not a New Testament word, nor is the word *archē*, 'rule', ever used of Church Authority. *Exousia*, 'authority' is used of the works and acts of Jesus himself many times; the Twelve also are given *exousia* to cast out demons, as in Mark 3.15, and St. Paul has *exousia* from the Lord 'for building up and not for casting down', 2 Cor. 10.8 and 13.10. But this authority is a *diakonia*, a ministry, just as Jesus himself came 'not to be ministered unto, but to minister', Matt. 20.25–8, Luke 22.25–7; in both cases his words begin with a criticism of the domineering rule of the 'kings of the Gentiles', and declare the vocation of the apostles to be 'ministers', 'servants'

---

[1] This paper was read at a private symposium or Conference at the Abbey of Le Bec in France, in 1961, and is published in the volume of papers there read entitled *Problems of Authority*, edited by J. M. Todd (Darton, Longman and Todd, 1962), pp. 119–50.

of the Lord and of his people. For the ground of all Authority in the Church is the Grace of God, God's saving mercy: 'God with us, God bending down to us, God given to us'; this Grace 'comes from God, to me, and for all'. Hence in the authority which the servants of the Lord hold there may be no *dominatio*, no possessiveness. Here is the very basis of Christian 'hierarchy'; it is all for service, on the part not only of church officers, but also of fathers and their children, masters and their slaves; for it applies to all human relationships. The 'horizontal' relations of men to one another all depend on their 'vertical' relation to God in Christ; they are not left in their natural or 'fleshly' reality, but are transformed 'in the Lord'. Yet, he says, very many Christians today have scarcely an inkling of this, and of the profound conversion which it presupposes (pp. 120–3).

In the period which follows, St. Ignatius of Antioch is thinking of this 'vertical' relation when he tells the Magnesians or Trallians that in obeying their bishop they are obeying God. The bishop's attitude to the people in the primitive Church is illustrated by the fact that in the liturgies the bishop-celebrant never prays as 'I', but always as 'we'; he prays in the name of all, as being spiritually one, and of one mind, with them. It is illustrated, again, by St. Cyprian's rule never to make a decision on the strength of his personal opinion without consulting his presbyters and deacons or without the approbation of the people. 'In the early church authority was that of men who were like princes in a community which was wholly sanctified, a *plebs sancta*, and overshadowed by the Spirit of God' (pp. 124–7).

This was the Age of Martyrs. New dangers arose with the Peace of the Church, when the Church had the active support of the civil power, when bishops ranked as senators, and when, with the slow breakdown of the organization of the Roman Empire, it fell to a bishop like St. Augustine to spend whole days in hearing civil cases and giving judgement. Still more, after the collapse of the Empire in the West the great churches and the monasteries were centres not only of godly life but also of civilization and learning. There was here great peril of secularization, and there was in fact much worldliness among Christians; and the monastic movement from the ascetics of the deserts onwards, has often been represented as a protest against this. But that is a one-sided view; the monastic movement was not so separate from the life of the Church. The superior of a monastic community was chosen because he was a man of God; and it was on this that his real authority depended, as a ruler of free men. It is to be noticed how many of the great bishops from the fourth to the sixth century were or had been monks. We need only remember such names as St. Basil, St. John Chrysostom, St. Augustine, St. Patrick, St. Gregory the Great; and even down to the twelfth century all the Archbishops of Canterbury were monks (p. 128–9). In the fifth century the bishop enjoyed great respect: this is illustrated by the words of a civil servant to him whom we know as Saint Ambrose: 'When the praetorian prefect Probus sent his subordinate Ambrose, then only a catechumen, to take up at Milan the post of *consularis*, he said to him, "Go and do your work not like a judge but like a bishop".' For the office of bishop 'represented a whole ideal of care for men's welfare, disinterestedness, welcome, in short an essentially moral ideal of authority' (p. 131).

Such was the pattern of life of great leaders such as St. Ambrose, St. Augustine, or St. Gregory the Great. For St. Gregory, 'servant of the servants of God' was very far from being a mere official phrase: 'he exercised his authority like a kind of supreme and universal Father Abbot', combining the 'tender care of a mother with the authority of a father'.[1] 'Not all the Popes have followed this course. Yet we should note that, if Rome succeeded in obtaining, over and above her power, the *authority* of her primacy, it was in large part due to the value and wisdom of her answers to all the questions which were put to her from every region of Christendom' (p. 132).

Thus the great bishops of this period were careful to relate authority to its transcendent spiritual principle and to preserve

[1] 'Curandum quippe est, ut rectorem subditis et matrem pietas et patrem exhibeat disciplina', St. Gregory's *Pastoral Rule*, II, 6.

its relation to the Church-community. 'At this period the primal and decisive reality in ecclesiology is still the *ecclesia* itself, that is, the totality, the community, the unity of the faithful. This may appear to be a truism; but ten years of study and of reflection on the history of the ecclesiastical doctrine have convinced me that it is not.' So St. Augustine says to his flock continually, *Vobis sum episcopus, vobiscum Christianus*—'To you I am your bishop, together with you I am a Christian', and 'a sinner together with you', and 'a disciple and a hearer of the Gospel together with you' (p. 132).

A change, however, came in the Hildebrandine period, with the Popes Leo IX (1049–59) and Gregory VII (1073–81), which is best illustrated by the two senses of the term *Vicar of Christ*. The first can be described as a 'vertical' relation of the holder of authority to his Lord, such that the Lord's word is present and operative in the man who holds authority in his Name. Such had been the authority of the Old Testament prophet, to whom the word of the Lord came; such was the authority of the apostles of Jesus, Matt. 10.40, Luke 10.16; and such we have seen to be the authority of the bishop in the mind of St. Ignatius of Antioch. As another Roman Catholic writer expresses it, it is not so much that the bishop possesses authority, but rather that authority possesses him, so that he forgets himself in his message.[1]

The other sense can be described as a 'horizontal' relation of the holder of authority to a representative who takes his place, and acts on his behalf, as if he were a plenipotentiary ambassador who acts in the name of his sovereign, but also is liable to be called to account on his return for his use of the power committed to him. (Such, we may remind ourselves, was the authority of the Jewish *shaliach*, 'so that the envoy's action unalterably committed the principal'; and here is the peril of that

[1] Prof. Fransen, S.J. of Louvain, in another paper in the same book *Problems of Authority*, p. 45. He writes: 'In matters of faith no man, not even the Pope or the bishops, possesses the truth. Christ himself, the Word of the Father, and the only "Way, truth and life", continually gives himself to his Church in the outpouring of his Spirit. This divine truth *possesses us*.' The neglect of this, he says, leads to all sorts of clericalism and legalism.

analogy for the Apostle of Jesus, or for the bishop.[1]) It did become the sin of the mediaeval church that importance came to be attached to 'the formal validity of authority, to its possession of a title in law', and that the word *ecclesia* came to denote 'not so much the body of the faithful as the system, the apparatus, the impersonal depositary of the system of rights whose representatives are the clergy, or as it is now called, the Hierarchy, and ultimately the Pope and the Roman Curia. It is a fact that "Church" is sometimes understood by the theorists of ecclesiastical power or of papal authority as indicating clerics, priests and the Pope. . . . Here is one example among hundreds which could be given: "The Church is given the task of feeding the flock of Jesus Christ." But the Church is herself this flock.' The change of meaning is serious. Authority was in peril of being viewed in a wrong way, as from the point of view of worldly power and not from that of the properly Christian conception of authority (pp. 140–1). All this led up to 'the thunderclap of October 31st, 1517', when Ninety-five Theses were nailed up on the door of the Church of All Saints, Wittenberg.

Biblical texts which referred to God's dealings with his people Israel could thus be perverted to support ecclesiastical power. Jer. 1.10, where the LORD says to the prophet, 'See, I have set thee this day over the nations and over kingdoms, to root up and to pull down, to waste and to destroy, and to build and to plant', could become an assertion of the supreme authority of the Pope and his right to depose kings. 1 Cor. 2.15, 'But the spiritual man judges all things, and he himself is judged by no man', and 6.3, 'Know you not that we shall judge

---

[1] *The Apostolic Ministry*, pp. 228 f., and p. 230 where Gregory Dix writes, 'The *shaliach's* action irrevocably commits even his divine principal: for God has conditioned himself by his own word of promise.' Gregory Dix forgets himself here. That sentence ought never to have been written without at least a reminder that the servant of the Lord is subject to the Lord's judgement. Compare pp. 47–8 above, where it is noted that the evangelist has placed the Petrine commission, Matt. 16.18–19, in a paragraph which ends with a double reference in vss. 27, 28 to the Lord's Advent when he shall render to every man—including every *shaliach*—according to his works.

angels? how much more, things of the world', could be inter-preted of the right of priests, and more especially and supremely of the right of the Pope, to judge secular powers (p. 138). Canon Law, which came more and more to dominate mediaeval thought, was to 'weave a kind of Noe's cloak around the prestige and honour of clerics, bishops and Roman dignitaries' (p. 135). 'Under these conditions, instead of being seen as a relationship of superior to subordinate *within* the vast system of mutual love and service between Christians, who are Christians as the result of a grace for which each is accountable to all, does not authority run the risk of being posited *first and foremost as authority for its own sake,* and so of being looked upon in a purely juridical and sociological way, and not from a spiritual and Christian standpoint? (p. 141).

This other side was never quite lost. Protests were made, again and again, 'in the more or less anti-ecclesiastical spiritual movements so frequent in the twelfth century, and which con-tinued in the Franciscan spiritual movement down to the fourteenth century, when it was succeeded by Lollardism and subsequently by the Hussite movement. All these . . . said the same thing: "Less pomp, and more of the Gospel! You are Constantine's Church, not the Church of the Apostles" ' (p. 142). A man of God such as Robert Grosseteste, Bishop of Lin-coln, could reply to the Pope: *Filialiter et obedienter non obedio, contradico et rebello,* 'In virtue of the filial obedience which I owe, I disobey, I reject what you say, and I resist.' (p. 143.)

The fault, however, did not lie only in the clergy. The Hilde-brandine reforms did assert the spiritual rights of the Church against a worldly laity. There was the Investiture Controversy, whether the right to confer bishoprics and invest the bishops-elect with staff and ring should be in the hands of the emperor. There were the *Eigenkirchen,* the 'private churches', founded and endowed by powerful laymen for the sake of the Church minis-tries which they needed, and owned and controlled by them. This led to an episode which is vividly described by T. M. Parker in his admirable essay on 'Feudal Episcopacy' in *The Apostolic Ministry*:

Authority in the Middle Ages

'In 1111, Pope Paschal II, an unworldly monk, proposed a drastic solution of the whole affair. If the emperor would renounce his claim to invest bishops, the Church for her part would give up all her temporalities, all the lands held feudally from the Crown, and the clergy would henceforth live merely upon the tithes and offerings. The bishops, as the Pope said, "would then be free from temporal cares, so as to give themselves to the care of their flocks and not to be absent any longer from their churches". Here at last was exposed starkly the problem which lay at the root of the matter. In an age when land was the sole source of wealth, the church, if she were to be endowed at all, must be endowed in land. But land was more in feudal times than a source of income: it was the basis of civil administration, and its holding on any large scale inevitably entangled the holder in civil affairs. If ecclesiastics were to be free from temporal ties, as the Hildebrandine party thought was essential for their spiritual duties and welfare, if unworthy pastors were to be kept out of bishoprics and other prelacies, they would have to cease to be landowners and live upon the charity of the faithful . . .

'The choice was made, we might almost say, at the moment when Paschal produced his drastic solution . . . When the proposed concordat was read in St. Peter's, it was received with indignant clamour by the ecclesiastics present, to whom it came as a thunderbolt; apostolic poverty held no attractions for them. And then the lay reaction was no less significant: the lay magnates present clamoured no less loudly against a concordat which would have deprived them all of their much-prized rights of patronage; the power of preferring to a see, an abbey, or a parish, a relative, a friend, or a man who might show them favour, was one which they were unwilling to forgo. The combined protests wrecked the scheme before it had begun, and the Pope was compelled to withdraw it. In that tumultuous scene in the ancient basilica the whole temper of the age stands revealed, and a choice was made no less momentous than on a similar occasion of which one is inevitably reminded, when another disorderly crowd

77

shouted for Barabbas—a crowd that equally was composed of both clerics and laymen. To say this is not to prejudge the issue: there are things to be said on both sides. Nevertheless, the choice when once made proved virtually irrevocable, and its consequences, which we now have to examine, were far-reaching. The form of the mediaeval episcopate was fixed. We have reached the term of a long process which had been working itself out since the conversion of Constantine.'[1]

Dr. Parker concludes the next section of his essay with the words: 'Was it surprising if the Reformers failed to see in the sixteenth-century prelate, as much temporal magnate as spiritual ruler, distracted by cares of State and local governmen, in juridical rather than personal relationship with his flock, the successor of an apostle?'[2]

(ii) *The Liturgy in the Middle Ages*

Liturgy is of quite central importance in the Church's life, since it is there that the Church knows herself to be the Church. By her nature the Church belongs to two worlds at once, to the world of social, economic and political life, and to the eternal World, to the Kingdom of God, to the divine Gospel of Jesus Christ. It is in Liturgy above all that the two worlds are seen meeting one another. It is true indeed that the study of Liturgy is often taken to be the study of liturgical texts. But the texts, the written and printed liturgies, are to the Liturgy itself only as the printed score of a symphony is to the actual performance of the symphony by an orchestra, and the share of the audience in it.

Liturgy is the action of the assembled Church, as the believing and worshipping People of God, meet together to adore and worship God, and to re-enact the mystery of man's redemption through the incarnation and death and resurrection of the Son of God. Hence the central act of Christian Liturgy is that of Easter Day, or rather of the night and day of Easter,

---

[1] *The Apostolic Ministry*, pp. 373–4. The preceding and the following pages give an excellent account of the secularization of the mediaeval Church.

[2] ibid., p. 384.

when the history of our redemption is commemorated as a series of historical events, and also made present in its living power. In its old form it includes baptism with confirmation, in which the newly-baptized members of the Church pass from darkness into light and become members of Christ, and all the baptized Christians renew their own baptism, and all together celebrate the *anamnesis* or memorial of their redemption which the Lord gave at the Last Supper, the memorial of the Accepted Sacrifice of the Son of God, and of his victory over the powers of darkness. Of the Eucharist as sacrifice, there will be more to say in a later chapter. Here we are concerned with liturgy, at this its central point, as the place where the Church is seen to be the Church, and the ordinary, common life of men, including all his social, economic and political life, is seen as redeemed to God.

In the Church of the early centuries each Lord's Day was a weekly Easter, and in each place the local church assembled to celebrate the Christian mystery. All the members of the Church had their part in the action; the bishop presided and rehearsed the Eucharistic Prayer, the presbyters were grouped round him, the deacons assisted and received the offerings which the people brought, of bread and wine and other gifts, and the people had their part in song and prayer, hearing the scriptures read in their own language, bringing their gifts at the Offertory, and receiving together the Communion of the body and blood of the Lord. The whole was the enactment of the Lord's own action when he *took* the loaf and *blessed* or gave *thanks*, and *broke* the loaf and *gave* it to them, and likewise the cup: these four verbs are expressed in the Offertory, the Consecration, the Fraction or breaking of the one loaf for Communion, and the Communion itself.

But while in the East the Church had a relatively stable history, till its troubles began with the Mohammedan and the Turkish invasions, the West was involved in all the troubles consequent on the fall of the Western Empire. We have seen how great its difficulties were as regards Authority: they were not less great in regard to Liturgy.

From Middle Ages to Reformation

First there was the problem of language. In the apostolic age, the Greek language was current throughout the Roman Empire, apart from the Syriac-speaking churches in the East; and till the latter half of the fourth century Greek was the language of the liturgy at Rome. The Church of Rome then changed over from Greek to Latin. The fine homiletic style of the sermons of St. Leo in the early-middle fifth century suggests that there was already a well-established liturgical Latin, besides the Latin Bible; and the *de sacramentis* of pseudo-Ambrose seems to prove that the change-over had taken place before 383. For several centuries the people of Rome could join happily in the Latin service.[1] But it was otherwise with the newly-converted barbarian tribes, especially north of the Alps. St. Cyril and St. Methodius did indeed set to work on a Slavonic translation of the Bible and the liturgy in Bohemia and Moravia: but that was one language among many, and the example was not followed in the West. Latin was the language in which the Bible was known, and the language of all who could read, all educated people, all the monasteries. The liturgy therefore remained in Latin, and this became and remained a difficulty for the ordinary lay people, especially among the tribes north of the Alps, who no longer understood what was sung and said in church.

Second, following on this, comes the loss by the people of an active share in the action of the service. From about the ninth century private masses became common, and the central part of the rite, the Canon or Eucharistic Prayer, came to be said in silence: there is evidence of this about 900, when orders were given to that effect. The Mass was thus coming to be thought of as the action of the celebrating priest, and the idea that the people had a share in the offering was dropping out. The Offertory-action in which the people themselves brought their

[1] 'The prayers were therefore said aloud. To this the Canon and the Words of Institution were no exception. With a solemn Amen—still retained today in the Amen immediately before the Paternoster—the whole congregation gave outward expression to the fact that they had heard and had taken part in praying the words of the Canon.'—Prof. Klauser, *The Western Liturgy and its History* (E. T. trans. F. L. Cross, Mowbray, 1952), p. 41.

bread and wine to the altar had lasted longest at Rome itself, but by the eleventh century this too had gone. We must remember that the conversion of the Western nations had been too rapid; whole tribes had followed the chiefs into the Church. There came the dropping away from Communion also, so that in 1215 the Lateran Council laid down once a year as an obligatory minimum. The central point of the action, in the popular view, now came to be the Elevation of the Host, which came in in the thirteenth century. People would go from one altar to another, many of them believing that if they saw the Host they would not die that day.

Third: The prevalence of the Arian heresy in parts of northern Europe called out on the part of the Church an emphasis on our Lord's divinity, which continued after the Arian peril was over; this was commonly a one-sided emphasis, and there came to be a loss of the truth that he is true Man and our Mediator, and that in the Liturgy we pray *to* the Father *through* the Son *in* the Holy Spirit. Instead, the common picture of our Lord was that of the mighty King who will be the Judge at the Last Day. This picture of our Lord was really Apollinarian or Monophysite, these being the two allied heresies which denied in effect his true manhood: and whenever this happens, we get a wrong idea about the Church and the Ministry also, so that the priest is thought of as an exalted personage who is on a level above that of ordinary men.

But the realization of our Lord's manhood was bound to come back; and when it did, in the late Middle Ages, it was in a one-sided way. Earlier, there had been the triumphal crucifix which made no attempt to be realistic, but depicted him as robed and crowned, victorious in his passion. Now came the realistic Crucifix, depicting the tortured Christ, and the *pieta* showing his dead body taken down from the Cross. What was missing was the 'Mystery of Christ', the glory of the risen Lord; what took its place was an individualistic piety, a personal religiousness—which in the Church of England today still leads people to desire the 'nice quiet service' at eight o'clock on Sunday, and to take their places in church by preference away

F   81

from their fellow-worshippers, at a service which is the successor of the private masses of the middle ages in being a clerical monologue. Then the priest said mass for the people; now he celebrates Holy Communion for them. This is a very different thing from the common prayer of the assembled Christian community. Yet our Prayer Book is called the 'Book of *Common* Prayer'. This religious individualism is one of the ways in which post-Reformation practice has perpetuated the faults of the middle ages.

Thus in a variety of ways the lay-people in the middle ages were being deprived of the share in the Liturgy, which properly belongs to them as the *plebs sancta*, the holy people of God. It was not merely that they were not living holy lives—for indeed they were not, as the copious moral exhortations in the Prayer Books of 1549 and 1552 are sufficient to prove; the ungodliness of the English people at that time lay as a heavy burden on the compilers of the Prayer Book. But there was a cause for this. It would seem that most of what we have said about the failures of the middle ages might be summed up under the heading of the Double Standard:[1] a high standard for those who lived in monasteries and the 'clerical' class generally who were educated and knew Latin—though there was much transgression among them also—and a lower standard for the layman in the world, who was indeed reckoned to be doing well if he kept clear of grave offences against the moral law. This gulf between the clerics and the illiterate lay-people remained, though great endeavours were made to overcome it, of which the typical instance is the evangelistic preaching of St. Francis and his friars. Yet they too became an Order, and were absorbed into the clerical system.

The great fault, or we may say, the heresy, of the Double Standard lay in a false doctrine of 'the holy'. It lay in the notion that the church building and the church service and the clergy are 'holy', and ordinary daily life is and always will be

---

[1] I have written a brief account of this Double Standard, based largely on K. E. Kirk, *The Vision of God*, in my book *God's Kingdom and Ours*. S.C.M. Press (1958), in the section entitled 'Clericalism', pp. 77–87.

'common and unclean'. This notion is a potent force making for evil in the Church today; and it is flatly heretical, since it is a denial of what is implied in the Incarnation of the Son of God in true human flesh, whereby that which is 'common' is purged of 'uncleanness' by being redeemed to God. This is the meaning of *Communio Sanctorum* in one of its senses, both of which are right and true: it means the communion or fellowship of 'the saints', the holy people of God,[1] and it also means 'the sharing in holy things', 'the commonness of holy things'—a meaning which is clearer in the Greek form of the phrase than in the Latin—so that what is 'common' is 'made holy'. So it was that Jesus consorted with publicans and sinners, not to condone their sin but to take it away; and so it was that the patristic church rejected the Gnostic heresy, because it denied that common daily life could be lived to God's glory, and so rejected marriage as defiling, and sought salvation in an escape from the body and its desires and lusts into an individualistic spirituality. This false doctrine of 'the holy' is the denial of the principle of the Incarnation, and of the sacraments, in which ordinary water is used for the washing-away of sin, and common bread and wine, the offerings of the laity, brought by them to the altar, are consecrated, and then received by them as the sacrament of the Body and Blood of Christ to preserve their bodies and souls unto everlasting life. The loss of the Communion of the People was the central fault of the Liturgy in the Middle Ages.

(iii) *Martin Luther, a Prophet of God*

In 1517 the storm broke. The Word of the Lord came to the Augustinian monk Martin Luther in the wilderness. Martin Luther was a Prophet of God; it is only when we see him as a prophet that we understand him aright.

He spoke the Word of the Lord in a day when the Means of Grace were being treated as a sacramental *system*; and that is a thing which it is always possible for us to do, just because God

---

[1] Cf. for this pp. 128–30 in Chapter VIII.

is ever present to save and help. The peril is that we can take Him for granted: we can depersonalize the word 'Grace', which in the New Testament is used to mean first God's saving Mercy, and then the presence and activity of God the Holy Spirit. When we depersonalize the word 'Grace', we can think of 'it' as available whenever we need it, much as the water in the pipes is there for us when we turn on the tap. So whenever the sacraments of God's Grace are made into a system, we are taking it for granted that grace is always available; and of course we add at once that it is necessary for us to approach the sacraments with right dispositions, with faith and penitence, and 'co-operate with grace'. Here is the favourite British sin of Pelagianism, for our 'co-operation' is an activity of our own in providing the necessary faith and repentance.

This was Martin Luther's agonizing problem, when as a zealous and earnest monk he tried his hardest to live a life well-pleasing to God. Everyone believed in the middle ages that God's grace was freely given, and everyone believed that God's Righteousness or Justice meant in the first place that he must punish sin. Luther, being a man with a most sensitive conscience, was aware that his efforts to bring to God a truly penitent heart were self-regarding efforts, with the aim of saving his soul and escaping God's wrath. Staupitz, the superior of his community, helped him much with spiritual counsel, and not least by setting him to study theology and give lectures on the Psalms and the New Testament epistles; but he could not answer all his questions.

Between 1513 and 1515 came the dawning of the light, and his liberation, by the discovery that the Righteousness of God in Holy Scripture means also his saving Mercy. God is good, and therefore he must punish sin: but also, God is good in saving sinful men, and this is just what he has done in the saving work of Jesus Christ. What Luther rediscovered was the Reality of God and his personal action in and through the means of Grace. Thus he broke clean away from the mischievous conception of the sacramental *system*: and when he saw and heard for himself that it was God the Saviour who came to him in the sacraments of Grace, faith and hope and joy came unsought, and with them liberation of spirit, so that he now found himself doing good works and keeping God's law happily and gladly.

Thus, as Professor Regin Prenter puts it, he learnt *not* to say, '*In order that* I may be saved, I must not only believe, but also do good works by co-operating with Grace for my salvation, for without such good works Grace cannot save me'; but: '*Because* I am already saved by Grace, through faith alone, therefore it becomes possible for me to do good works, to praise God and help my neighbour. Apart from these good works, Grace has saved me already, and thereby they can be *good* works, since they are not done for my own sake, to co-operate with grace for my own salvation, but for God's sake and for his glory, and for my neighbour's sake, for his good, as God has commanded.'[1]

So Luther himself wrote in his brief Autobiography in 1545:

'At last, God being merciful, as I meditated day and night on the connection of the words [cf. Rom. 1.17], namely: "The Justice of God is revealed in it, as it is written 'The just shall live by faith' ", then I began to understand the justice of God as that by which the just lives by the gift of God, namely by faith. . . . This straightway made me feel as though re-born, and as though I had entered through open gates into Paradise itself. From then on, the whole face of Scripture appeared different. I ran through the Scriptures, then, as memory served, and found the same analogy in other words, as, the Work of God, that which God works in us; the Power of God, with which he makes us strong, the Wisdom of God with which he makes us wise, the Fortitude of God, the Salvation of God, the Glory of God. And now, as much as I had hated this "Justice of God" before, so much the more sweetly I extolled this word to myself now, so that this place in Paul was to me as a real gate of paradise. Afterwards I read Augustine "On the Spirit and the Letter",

---

[1] Prenter, *Reformatoren Martin Luther*. Forlaget Aros, Denmark (1960), pp. 34–5. Regin Prenter is Professor at Aarhus University in Denmark, and his name is an honoured one in Scandinavia and Germany.

where beyond hope I found that he also similarly interpreted the Justice of God: that with which God endows us, when he justifies us.'[1]

Luther says in his great Preface to his Lectures on the Epistle to the Romans:

'This Epistle is the central point of the New Testament, and the clearest expression of the Gospel. Therefore it is worth while that a Christian man should not only know it all by heart, but daily ponder on it as the soul's daily bread. It can never be learnt or studied too much; the more one works upon it, the more precious it becomes and the better it tastes. . . . The first thing is to get a clear understanding of the key-words, and know what Paul means by them: Law, Sin, Grace, Faith, Righteousness, Flesh, Spirit, etc.: otherwise the reading is no help. . . . "Law" does not mean a statement of things that are to be done and not done, as it is with human laws, which a man may obey though his heart is not in it. . . . If you obey the law for fear of punishment or desire for reward, then you do so without any love for the law, and you would wish to act quite otherwise if the law were not there. Inwardly, therefore, you hate the law. . . . No: to "fulfil the law" is to do what it commands with joy and love, not from compulsion. . . . This joy of a free love is what the Holy Spirit puts into our hearts.

'And so Faith is not belief in human dreams and ideas, as some thing . . . as if faith were an idea in their minds. No: Faith is God's own work in us; it transforms us and brings new life, it slays the Old Adam and makes us in our hearts new men. . . . Faith is a living, mighty, active, powerful thing, so that it is impossible that it should not lead to good works. It does not ask whether we ought to do good works, but while the question is being asked it has already done them, and is always thus busy. . . .'[2]

---

[1] Translation from Gordon Rupp, *The Righteousness of Faith*, p. 122.

[2] This is a free rendering from Prenter, *Reformatoren Martin Luther*, p. 28. For the full text, see *Reformation Writings of Martin Luther*. E.T. by B. Lee Wolff (Lutterworth Press), Vol. II, pp. 284–5 and 288.

A Prophet of God

It is not true, then, to say that Luther was an antinomian, and held that the Gospel abolishes the Law, so that the Christian is now free to do just what he likes. He did not teach this, any more than St. Paul taught that a person might continue in sin that grace might abound (Romans 6.1 ff.). Nor did he deny the need of sanctification: he believed in the Holy Spirit; his *simul justus et pecutor* can be described as a rendering of Romans Chapter 7. Luther refused always to identify Sin with acts of sin which can be tabulated according to the rules given by Moral Theology. Sin, *hamartia*, is the Old Adam which is always present with us, the love of Self, the Ego which is *incurvatus in se*, 'twisted inwards towards the Self'. Thus the Christian is continually sinning, and continually being forgiven and healed. Luther could take 'the Forgiveness of Sins' as the summary statement of the work of Grace, and here he was profoundly right; but he has been liable to be misunderstood by people who take the Forgiveness of Sins as the absolution of particular sins after confession.

Luther had found again the key to the Gospel of God and to the New Testament; in his prophetic word it came alive. For the German people too it came alive, and he was amazed at the way in which the people flocked to hear the Gospel proclaimed. One of the immediate fruits of the Reformation was that the people began again to sing in church; Luther gave them not only the Bible in their own language, but also the splendid melodies and words of his chorales. Professor Prenter says of him:

'At the back of the Reformation there stood a great man, of rich spiritual experience and deep thought. But it was not *his* greatness as a man, not *his* experiences, not *his* thoughts, that started the Reformation. It was the *Scripture*, which had opened itself up to a sorely tempted man battling for his soul's salvation: as he himself said: "I stood up against the Pope, the Indulgences and all the papists, but *I* had no power. All that I did was to go ahead and preach and write God's word: otherwise I did nothing. And while I slept or drank Wittenberg beer with my Philip and Amsdorf, the Word brought it about that the Papacy became weak, and no prince or emperor could have had power to do it so much harm. It was not I: it was the Word that did and achieved all this. . . . I have done nothing, only left the Word to do its work. What do you imagine the Devil thinks?. . . . He sits in Hell and thinks: 'O, the fools have made a fine mess of me!' But the one thing that harms him is when we set to with the Word. That alone is mighty and takes men's hearts captive." [1]

Thank God, we have had our Evangelicals in the Church of England to bear witness that Luther was a prophet of God. Thank God, we also know now that the true Catholic is he who is also an Evangelical; and thank God, the contagion is spreading, so that Roman Catholics are studying St. Paul, and learning to study Luther also and find out what his message really was. But prophets must expect to have a bad time: they have enthusiastic followers, and they have also those who build their tombs and falsify their message. This may be studied in Gordon Rupp's great book, *The Righteousness of Faith*, the first part of which, pp. 3–77, is devoted to 'The Historians' Luther'. Later Lutherans found Luther too much for them and devised a Lutheran orthodoxy with a rigid system of doctrines which everyone must believe if he would be saved. On the other side, we have had the learned but mischievous biographies of Luther by Denifle and Grisar, by which even Maritain was led astray in his *Three Reformers* (1932): but Lortz was much better, and since then we have had Bouyer with his *Spirit and Forms of Protestantism*.[2] In England, the older Anglo-Catholics, observing that the German Lutherans had no bishops, labelled him as a heretic, and we have in general left him on one side. Dr. Mascall in his *Recovery of Unity* makes much of Bouyer's accusation that Luther was a Nominalist, but scarcely notices his exposition of Luther's positive message. Yet the saintly Anglo-Catholics of the eighteenth century were deeply Evangelical at heart; Fr. Stanton had in his study all the works of Spurgeon.

[1] Prenter, *Reformatoren Martin Luther*, pp. 10–11.
[2] E.T., published by Harvill (1956).

A Prophet of God

It is plainly impossible for us in this book to deal with the various Protestant confessions, each of which has had its own insights, its experiences and its history. We have dealt with Luther because he was the prophet of the Reformation, and with him it began. Calvin was deeply different from Luther, for he was a great systematic theologian, as Luther certainly was not. Calvin set out a new church order; Luther did not, since his endeavour was to reform the old order. Yet Calvin's intention was still to build on the old foundations, and especially to reform the pastoral ministry of the Church and its care of souls. Luther, on the other hand, stood far more on the traditional lines. He always maintained his belief in the real presence of the Lord in the Eucharist, as in his conflict with Zwingli; he attached great importance to 'the power of the keys' in sacramental confession and absolution; and in the Lutheran churches the old introits and the chants of the proper of the Mass, such as the *Sanctus*, continued to be sung in Latin for a century and more after his death, the scriptural lessons being, of course, in the vernacular.

Two important problems, however, he can be said to have left unsolved, that of Sacrifice in the Eucharist, and that of the Ministry; and they have remained unsolved by Protestantism generally. We shall have to deal with these in some detail in subsequent chapters, and show how it has not been till our own day that the hope has arisen of an agreed answer to these controversial questions.

Luther attacked vigorously the current doctrine and practice of Eucharistic Sacrifice. As regards doctrine, the Latin Ordinal had contained for perhaps three centuries the delivery of the chalice and paten to the newly ordained priest, with the commission to offer sacrifice to God for the living and the dead; and as regards practice, the numberless chantry masses, especially for the souls of the departed, seemed to indicate that each Mass was a separate sacrifice, offered by men to God. To Luther it seemed that the Latin Canon of the Mass was full from end to end of a false doctrine of sacrifice, apart from the Words of Institution, which spoke of God's saving Grace. These,

89

From Middle Ages to Reformation

therefore, he retained in his revised rites, omitting the prayers which in the old canon had preceded and followed them. To this day the Lutheran Churches have no worthy Eucharistic Prayer, and it is only quite recently that endeavours are being made to repair this fault.[1]

Nor can Luther be said to have given a satisfactory doctrine of the Ministry. As we shall see in Chapter VIII, he believed that the Ordained Ministry was of divine ordinance, being based on the Lord's calling of the Apostles; and he vigorously proclaimed the Universal Priesthood of All Christians. He found both these in the New Testament; but he can scarcely be said to have made it clear how they are related to one another. That he rejected Episcopacy was not surprising, for as we noticed on page 78, the bishops of his day had no desire to behave like successors of the Apostles. But it was certainly not a valid argument for the total rejection of episcopacy, that existing bishops behaved like prelates; yet he did know better, for he knew very well what had been the pattern of episcopacy in St. Augustine and St. Gregory the Great.

Did he not also err when he despaired of the Church of Rome, and identified the Pope with Antichrist? There was perhaps more excuse here, for he firmly believed that he was living in the last days, and the Final Advent of the Lord was very near: hence his use of the term 'Antichrist'. But he did not foresee that there might one day be a Pope John XXIII, who would not be rejected without a hearing as was Paschal II, but would be supported by a great and growing revival within the Roman Catholic Church, with new translations of the Bible, a serious study of the Bible as the Word of God by millions of Catholics, a great liturgical movement, and a keen ecumenism.

[1] There is a good eucharistic prayer, for instance, in the new *Service-book* issued in 1958 by the American Lutheran Churches, though the bare recital of the Words of Institution stands as a permitted alternative; and there is an excellent one in a German eucharistic rite, which is possibly the best of all the revised liturgies which we have had. The text of this is from the *Agende* of Karl Bernhard Ritter, and it is published as a booklet entitled *Evangelische Messe* by the Johannes Stauda-Verlag, Kassel, Germany, 2nd. edn., 1959.

CHAPTER VI

Priesthood and Sacrifice in the Scriptures

*

In the remaining chapters of this book we must draw together the threads of our discussion, and state our questions and reach some conclusions.

We have completed now a historical survey as far as the Reformation and Martin Luther the father of the Reformation. In the sixteenth century the attempts that were made to reach a mutual understanding between Catholics and Protestants ended in failure: there followed controversial polemic, persecutions on both sides, and religious wars, till at last both sides settled down to an uneasy coexistence. 'Toleration' began to be a virtue; yet to tolerate one another is no fulfilment of the New Testament command to love one another, and in fact the different 'churches' became like fortified camps manned by theologians who demolished one another's arguments.

But at last, and particularly in this twentieth century, a wholly different attitude of Christians to one another has appeared; we speak now of a New Reformation both of the Reformation itself and of the Counter-reformation. There is a movement of mutual approach, which is seen to be closely related to the world-wide evangelistic mission of the Church as much in the European lands as in Asia and Africa. Three outward marks of this movement are, first the new biblical study, which while using modern critical exegesis seeks the Word of God in the Scriptures: then the liturgical movement, which sees the whole People of God as a *plebs sancta*, and restores to the laity their part in the Church's worship: and the ecumenical movement, which aims at the healing of the schisms which divide Christians.

With this in view, we must deal with what have been in the past two principal storm-centres of controversy, the doctrines of Sacrifice and of Priesthood. In this chapter we must consider these in Holy Scripture, and see how the Old Testament is fulfilled in the New; and then in Chapter VII, Sacrifice in relation to the Eucharist; in Chapter VIII the Priesthood of All Christians in relation to that of the Ordained Ministry, and in Chapter IX the prospect of the coming Unity.

(i) *Priesthood and Sacrifice in the Old Testament*

It is commonly assumed that the primary function of a priest is to offer sacrifice. So too the definition of a highpriest's function in Hebrews 5.1, is 'that he may offer gifts and sacrifices for sins'. But we know now that it was not so in the earlier Old Testament period, roughly down to the Exile. It was the centralization of sacrifice to the One Lord at the one altar, first in Josiah's Reform and Deuteronomy, and then in Ezra's Reform and the Priestly Code, that associated the priests with the Jerusalem temple, and made the sacrificial ritual their chief work.

But in the earlier period sacrifice could be offered anywhere, not indeed by anyone who chose to do so, but by the father of a family such as Manoah in Judges 13.16–19, by the head of a clan or tribe, such as Jephthah, Judges 11.31, 39, or by king Solomon, 1 Kings 8.62–3. Besides this, each sanctuary such as Shiloh and Bethel had its priests, who performed the ritual there. In Judges 17 and 19 we read of a young Levite being kidnapped by the Danites, who had been driven out of their inheritance by the Philistines, to be the priest of their sanctuary at the new Dan in the far north (18.11–31). After Levi had ceased to exist as a territorial tribe, it became the priestly tribe.

In the Blessing of Levi in Deut. 33, the priestly functions are

In the Old Testament

summed up as first to manipulate the sacred Oracle, then to give *Torah*, and only in the third place to offer sacrifice.

> *Give to Levi thy Thummim*
> *and thy Urim to thy godly one . . .*
> *For they observed thy word,*
> *and kept thy covenant.*
> *They shall teach Jacob thy ordinances,*
> *and Israel thy Law.*
> *They shall put incense before thee,*
> *and whole burnt-offerings upon thy altar.*
> (Deut. 33, 8a, 9b–10.)

The giving of *Torah* is also emphasized in the post-exilic prophet Malachi. In 1. 6–14, he castigates the priests for presuming to offer in the sacrifices polluted food, and blind, lame or diseased animals, and so profaning the temple services. Then in 2, 5–9 he says that Levi feared the LORD and

> *True instruction was in his mouth,*
> *He walked with me in peace and uprightness,*
> *And he turned away from iniquity.*
> *For the lips of a priest should speak knowledge,*
> *And men should seek instruction from his mouth,*
> *For he is a messenger of the LORD of hosts.*

This is the old tradition from before the exile, when the priests were the exponents of God's Law, and therefore judges who had to settle legal problems (such as the case of unintentional homicide in Deut. 17.8–13), and givers of *Torah* also in the sense of spiritual instruction and guidance in the way of obedience to God in daily life.

What, then, is the meaning of the 'priesthood of all Israel' in Exod. 19.5?

'Now therefore, if you will obey my voice, and keep my covenant, you shall be my own possession among all peoples; for all the earth is mine, and you shall be to me a kingdom of priests, and a holy nation.'

Plainly this does not mean that each and every Israelite could

93

function as a priest in offering sacrifice, but rather that Israel corporately is the LORD's possession or inheritance; all nations belong to him, but Israel is set apart as a royal priesthood. The promise is conditional upon Israel's loyal obedience to the LORD in her covenant-relation with him. The meaning must be that as the Levitical priesthood is the guardian of the *Torah* and the proclaimer of it, so Israel as a nation is called to be the guardian of the *Torah* of the LORD who is King and the witness of it to other nations; for Israel's faith and worship and way of life were what marked her off as different from other nations, and were the common possession of Israelites as such. This laid on each Israelite a personal responsibility, to be faithful to the Covenant which belonged to them all. We shall come later to the Universal Priesthood of all Christians, in 1 Peter 2, 5 and 9, and Rev. 1.6; 6.10; 20.6. We must consider then whether these passages are to be interpreted on the same lines as Exod. 19.5–6, so that the thought is that the whole Church-community is entrusted with the Christian *Torah*, which is the Gospel. But the offering of sacrifice, in its Christian meaning, will also come in.

The ritual of Sacrifice consisted of three parts: *Oblation*, when the offerer 'drew near' with his animal and/or cereal offering; laid his hand on the animal's head, and killed it; *Transformation*, when the priest threw or sprinkled or poured out the blood, and burnt part of the body or the whole body on the altar; and *Reconciliation*, when in some sacrifices priest and people joined in the sacrificial feast.

There were three types of Sacrifice: (a) the 'Peace-Offering' (*shelem*) and 'Sacrifice of Thanksgiving' (*todah*), which ended with the sacrificial feast. This was the case at the three agricultural festivals (Deut. 16), of Unleavened Bread (Passover), Weeks (Pentecost), and the Autumn Festival of the 'Ingathering' (Tabernacles); three times in the year Israel assembled to 'rejoice before the LORD'. The Passover, the annual memorial of the Deliverance from Egypt, was always kept as a family feast; and so it is still kept today in Jewish homes (the *Seder*), but now there can be no paschal lamb. The most common type of sacrifice in the earlier period was the sacrificial feast, such as that which Samuel in 1 Sam. 9 celebrated in a village with some thirty guests present, and in 1 Sam. 16 the family-sacrifice of Jesse and his sons. In the Psalms there are a number of allusions to the Sacrifice of Thanksgiving, such as Ps. 27.6, 'an oblation with great gladness', or Ps. 116.12–19, 'What shall I render unto the LORD for all that he has done to me? I will take the cup of salvation', 'pay my vows unto the LORD', 'offer the sacrifice of thanksgiving' 'in the courts of the house of the LORD'. The title of Ps. 100 (*Jubilate*) is 'A psalm for the Thank-offering'. The note of all this is joy and thanksgiving for the Covenant of God with men, his presence among them and his blessings bestowed on them, and their union with him and with one another.

(b) Then there was the 'Whole-burnt-offering' (*'olah*), in which the whole body of the victim was burnt, so that its fragrance might ascend to God 'for an odour of a sweet smell', and so there was no 'communion' of priest or people. This became specially prominent after the great Temple had been built at Jerusalem; and the Priestly Code gives in Exod. 29.38–46 directions for the daily burnt-offering of a lamb every morning and evening. The commentary there is that the Temple is the place 'where I will meet with you, to speak there to you', and 'I will dwell among the people of Israel, and will be their God'. The note here is that of man's homage to the transcendent God, his offering of adoration. But for the offerer, sacrifice had now become more remote.

(c) There was the 'Guilt-offering' (*'asham*) and the Sin-offering (*chattath*), in which there was no 'communion' of the offerers, but only of the priest. The note was the propitiation of God's wrath and the expiation of man's sin. The great annual act of Sin-offering was the Day of Atonement, Lev. 16.1–10 and 11–34, for the offences of all Israel. Yet because Israel knew that no sacrificial ritual, but only God's mercy, could secure the forgiveness of sins, the second goat over which the sins had been confessed was not sacrificed, but was taken away into the wilderness as the Scape-goat. The Day of Atonement, with the thought of Propitiation, held an important place in the religion of the later Judaism, and received some emphasis in the Epistle to the Hebrews. Thereby the Sin-offering came to set the tone of much of the late-mediaeval and Reformation theology of sacrifice.

The New Testament interpretation of Sacrifice depends very much, however, on the criticisms of the current sacrificial worship made by prophets and psalmists. The prophets denounced so severely the worship which they saw going on (e.g. Amos 5.21-6, Micah 6.3-8, Jer. 7.21-3), that in the 'Liberal' period many scholars believed that God wanted the sacrifices to stop altogether; it could be said that '*Jahvé will keinen Kult*', or that all that he wanted was good solid morality. But modern Protestant scholarship takes a far more sympathetic view, and sees that sacrifice was a vital part of the religion of Israel; indeed, when the sacrifices are condemned in Isa. 1.11-19, the Sabbath-keeping and the prayers are condemned with it.

The prophets denounce the worshippers, people who seek in effect to take out insurance-policies against the effect of their sins, so that they can go on sinning at their pleasure, as especially in Jer. 7.1-15. Amos condemns the shallow nationalism of his day: Hosea, the following of the Canaanite nature-religions; Isaiah, the foreign cults which came in during the terrible 'war of nerves' when people were terrified of the Assyrian menace (e.g. 28.11-18). In thus denouncing the worshippers, the prophets are vindicating the holiness of the sacrifices which are being profaned.

But the prophets and psalmists did also criticize sacrifice itself. They were asking, 'What does God really want from men?' And the answer could only be that, just as God does not need to be provided with food to eat (Ps. 50.9-15), so he does not need the animal-offerings which men make (Micah 6.6-8). What he does seek is the worship, obedience and love of man himself (Ps. 40.6-8; 69.30-33). Here we may notice that in the story of the sacrifice of Israel, in Gen. 22, it is suggested that the ritual itself does not answer to what is needed. In v. 7 the boy asks his father, 'Where is the lamb for a burnt-offering?'

Abraham replies, 'God will provide himself the lamb for a burnt offering, my son.' But what is provided in v. 13 is not a lamb, but a ram. The point is suggested only and not clearly stated; yet surely it was not lost on St. John, whom nothing escaped, when he wrote the words, 'Behold the Lamb of God', the lamb which God has provided. There is a whole sheaf of meanings in John 1.29: but the allusion to 'God will provide himself a lamb', Gen. 22. 8, is surely one of them.

There are two more high points in the Old Testament criticism of the sacrifices. Psalm 51 has a number of quasi-sacrificial phrases: 'cleanse me from my sin', 'purge me', 'deliver me from blood-guiltiness' (vv. 2, 7, 14): but at last he says outright in vv. 16–17:

> *For thou hast no delight in sacrifice;*
> *were I to give a burnt-offering, thou would'st not be pleased.*
> *The sacrifice acceptable to God is a broken spirit;*
> *a broken and contrite heart, O God, thou wilt not despise.*

This is a pointer to the reality which was, when God's time came, to interpret the symbolism of the slain animal. No man had such penitence to bring, till Christ came, the perfect Penitent on behalf of sinful men.

The second is in Isa. 53.10: 'when he makes himself (*or*, when thou makest him) an offering for sin', an *'asham*, a Guilt-offering. The Servant of the LORD has borne the sins of men (vv. 4–6, 12) in his wholly surrendered life and his martyrdom (vv. 8–9), and he is God's accepted sacrifice (v. 10). There is here no priest and no sacrificial ritual: but there is here the reality which the sacrifices symbolized, and there is here that which the prophets and psalmists said that God wanted of man. But who is the Servant? We are not told; but since the sacrifice for sin here described is universal in its scope—for, as Dr. Jeremias has shown,[1] the word 'many' in Isa. 53.11 and 12 does not mean 'some men but not all', but is equivalent to the

---

[1] See J. Jeremias, *The Eucharistic Words of Jesus*, pp. 148–52, on the words 'for many' in Mark 14.24.

word 'all' in v. 6, as it is in Romans 6.18 and 19—those exegetes are surely right who see here a prophecy of the Final Deliverance for man, to which the prophets of the Exile looked forward. The New Testament commentary on Isa. 53 is given in 1 Peter 1.10–12.

(ii) *The High-priesthood and the Sacrifice of Jesus Christ*

In the Old Testament sacrifices, and those of other ancient religions, there had been a sense that *somehow*, through a costly offering of a victim without blemish, and through blood-shedding and death, there was at last to be a way for man back to peace with God. In the Apostolic Preaching it was announced that this had taken place through the death and the resurrection of Jesus Christ. But this had not happened through the sacrifices offered by the Jerusalem priesthood. There had been a Fulfilment, to the meaning of which the prophets' criticisms of the sacrifices had contributed.

It is noteworthy that the connections of Jesus and his apostles with the religion of Judaism were far more with the Synagogue than with the Temple. He preached often in synagogues; so did St. Paul in every place to which he went, till he proclaimed that the Crucified One was the Messiah, and then there was a riot, and he was turned out. The early Christians worshipped in synagogues till they were expelled; thus the early part of the Christian liturgy was based on the Sabbath services of the synagogue. When He, and they, attended the temple services, it was always as 'laymen', as when in Acts 3.1, Peter and John were on their way to the prayers which preceded the afternoon Burnt-offering when they healed a lame man and a series of incidents followed, and Paul in Acts 21.26–7 was completing in the temple his Nazarite vow (Acts 18.18 and 21, 23–4) when there was a riot and he was arrested. Neither he nor they ever officiated in the temple. Jesus 'was not a priest', as is said in Heb. 8, 4: for 'a priest' was 'a male member of a priestly family': such were 'the priests who became obedient to the faith' according to Acts 6.7, but they did not rank as priests of the Church. The word 'priest' is nowhere used in the New Testament as a title of a Minister in the Church.

Jesus did indeed cleanse the temple shortly before his passion, and this meant and was understood to mean that he claimed authority over it.[1] But as he cleansed the temple he quoted the prophecy 'My house shall be called a house of prayer for all nations' (Mark 11.17), plainly looking forward to what the Temple in God's coming Kingdom would be. He was also accused at his trial of having said that he would destroy the temple made with hands and replace it with another made without hands (Mark 14.58); this saying is quoted in John 2.19 in the form 'Destroy this temple, and in three days I will raise it up', and many have thought that this is a more authentic version. In John 2.21 the evangelist adds 'But he spake of the temple of his body', that is to say, the body that was to rise from the dead, and also the Church which was to be his body. In all this, the eschatological character of his references to the temple is clear: the thought is not of the temple which Herod built—for he certainly predicted that this would be destroyed, as in Mark 13.2—but of the 'fulfilment' of the Temple in what the Book of Revelation calls the New Jerusalem, and in the Church-community which is repeatedly in the New Testament pictured as the Temple of God.[2]

Similarly, the death of Jesus on the cross was not a ritual action comparable to the Jewish sacrifices; it was his public execution as a criminal. But the meaning of it, in the light of the resurrection, was that God was here winning his *victory* over all the powers of evil, reclaiming man from the power of Satan and setting him free; that God was in Christ *reconciling* the world to himself, by the supreme act of divine love; that God was *recreating* that which he had created, by the work of the New Adam; and that here was the *Accepted Sacrifice*, delivering man from guilt and bringing him back to communion with God.

If Dr. Jeremias is right in holding that the Last Supper was the

---

[1] Cf. Hebert, *The Christ of Faith and the Jesus of History.* S.C.M. (1962), pp. 90–2.

[2] p. 49 above.

meal which was part of the Passover Sacrifice,[1] the old sacrificial order and the new there stood side by side; and he thinks that in the *Haggada* which Jesus must have recited he spoke of himself as the true Passover lamb.[2] In any case the reference in the narratives to the New Covenant which had been foreseen in Jeremiah 31.31–4 as that which should supersede the Covenant of Sinai, implies that the New Covenant also would require an act of sacrifice to inaugurate it.

Dr. T. W. Manson wrote thus about our Lord's priesthood and sacrifice:[3]

'For the author of Hebrews the high-priestly ideal is fulfilled, not by the ecclesiastical potentates of Jerusalem, but by the "high-priest after the order of Melchizedek", of whom he says that "he had to be made like unto his brethren in all respects, so as to be a merciful and faithful high-priest in matters for which they were answerable to God, to expiate the sins of the people. For as he himself has suffered under trials, he is able to help those who are undergoing trials" (Heb. 2.17–18). This latter point is further stressed in 4.15, where we are told that "we do not have a high-priest incapable of sympathizing with our weaknesses, but one who has been tried and tested in every respect as we are, yet is free from sin."

'Here we have the essential characteristics of a perfect high-priesthood: on the one side, an unbreakable link with God the Father, in the unfailing obedience of his Son; on the other, an unbreakable link with his fellow-men through an unfailing sympathy and understanding. This solidarity with God and man uniquely fits Christ to be the Mediator, to represent God to man and man to God, to make the Holy One of Israel real to his children, and to fit those sinful children to enter into the divine presence.

'The means by which this is effected is a sacrifice. And

[1] J. Jeremias, *The Eucharistic Words of Jesus*. S.C.M. (1958).

[2] Cf. 1 Cor. 5.7, where St. Paul says this; Jeremias, p. 144.

[3] T. W. Manson, *Ministry and Priesthood, Christ's and Ours*. Epworth Press (1958), pp. 58 ff.

here it is necessary to remind ourselves—we cannot do it too often—that sacrifice in the Bible is a *religious* act, and that we shall never come to its deepest significance by bringing in ideas devised from the theory and practice of Western criminal law. The main points made in Hebrews are these: (a) Christ the high-priest sacrifices himself, the perfect priest making the unblemished offering (7.26–7; 9.11; 14; 10.10). (b) This sacrificial act, in sharp contrast to the continually repeated sacrifices of the Temple ritual, takes place once for all. It is unique and unrepeatable. (c) At the same time the sacrifice is not to be thought of merely as an isolated event which occupied a few hours of time in the first third of the first century of our era. The priesthood of Christ is an eternal priesthood . . . (cf. the references to Ps. 110.4, and Hebrews 7). . . . The offering once made is perpetually effective and constantly operative. (d) The sacrifice . . . has the twofold character which belongs to placular sacrifice in the Jewish ritual: it is an *'asham*, a compensatory offering to God for wrongs done; and it is also a means of expiation, whereby the things in man which make it impossible for him to come into God's presence are removed or neutralized.'

He goes on to explain that the compensatory offering to God for man's disobedience is 'total obedience', as is set out in Psalm 40.6–8: 'Lo, I come to do thy will, O God' *is* the sacrifice of Christ, Heb. 10.5–10. Then he goes on to speak of the effect on sinful man. This rests on the unbreakable link of the High-priest with his fellow-men, his sympathy with them and his mercy on their failures. And so:

'It will not do to create artificial distinctions between the self-sacrifice of Christ and the self-sacrifice of Christians. For obedience is one and indivisible, love is one and indivisible, compassion is one and indivisible. We conserve the uniqueness of the high-priesthood of Christ, not by shutting it away in splendid isolation, but by declaring and demonstrating its power to create and comprehend in itself a true priesthood of believers, whose priestly service is taken up into and made part of his supreme sacrifice.'

All this exposition by a distinguished Presbyterian scholar is very good indeed; but he shows very plainly that he belongs to the Reformed traditions, by his emphasis on the Sin-offering. And though on pp. 66–7 of his book he goes on to speak disparagingly of the tendency which soon appeared in the primitive Church to speak of the Eucharist as a sacrifice, and to criticize the language in which Tertullian, Hippolytus and Cyprian spoke of the bishop as a high-priest ('so that the Christian bishop takes the place of the Jewish priest') yet he says on pp. 70–1:

'The focus of this high-priestly work in which Christ and his people share is the sacrament of the Eucharist. Here Christ-in-his-Church renews the gift of God's love to his people. Here Christ-in-his-Church which is his body, offers to God his-Church-in-himself on the altar of self-sacrifice, with the ritual of obedience and love. Let that be deemed a valid Eucharist in which Christ carries on the high-priestly task which is his alone.'

(iii) *The Priesthood of All Believers*

The most important texts here are those of 1 Peter 2:

'So come to him, our living Stone—the stone rejected by men, but choice and precious in the sight of God. Come and let yourselves be built, as living stones, into a spiritual temple; become a holy priesthood, to offer spiritual sacrifices acceptable to God through Jesus Christ' (vv. 4–5).

'But you are a chosen race, a royal priesthood, a dedicated nation, and a people claimed by God for his own, to proclaim the triumphs of him who has called you out of darkness into his marvellous light. You are now the people of God, who once were not his people; outside his mercy once, you have now received his mercy' (vv. 9–10).[1]

Here, vv. 4–5 echo what has been said earlier in 1. 15–16, where the text from Leviticus is quoted, 'Ye shall be holy, as I am holy'. The Christians, baptized into Christ and united with

---

[1] For the text, see the footnote on p. 131.

him in the Communion, are 'to offer spiritual sacrifices' in virtue of their union with him. For this is what sacrifice means, as it is fulfilled in Jesus Christ. It is an offering of sacrifice that takes place in liturgy first, and then in life: for the liturgy is there in order to set the course for the life to be lived out in the world, among men.

In vv. 9–10, the other idea of Priesthood as Guardianship of the *Torah* also comes in, especially in the phrase 'to proclaim the triumphs of him who has called you'. The word *aretas* is translated in A.V. and R.V. as 'excellencies', but in R.S.V. as 'wonderful deeds', and in N.E.B. as 'triumphs', i.e. in the proclamation of the mighty Acts of God. This Proclamation or Recital appears many times in the Old Testament, as very notably in the 'Great Hallel', Ps. 136, where the leader recites the mighty acts of the LORD, first in creation and then in the Exodus and the Entry into the Promised Land, and the people respond to each phrase *ki l'olam chasdō*, 'for his steadfast love endures for ever'. There always has been and there is today a great recital of the Lord's mighty acts in the Haggada recited at the Passover meal in the Jewish home. There is a similar recital in the Eucharistic Prayer of the old liturgies, finding its noblest expression in the Liturgy of St. Basil. Thus the Christians in 1 Peter are 'priests' in the older Old Testament sense also, since they know how to proclaim the triumphs of the Lord.

For further exposition of the meaning of the Priesthood of All Christians, we turn to other passages in the epistles. Ephesians 5.2 connects the duty of Christian love with Christ's own sacrifice:

'As God's dear children, try to be like him, and live in love as Christ loved you, and gave himself up for you as an offering and sacrifice whose fragrance is pleasing to God.'

The last phrase is that which is regularly used in the Old Testament of the whole-burnt-offering: 'for savour of a sweet smell'.

Then there is Romans 12.1–2, which connects the sacrificial self-giving of Christians with the common life of the Church-community as the Body of Christ.

'Therefore, my brothers, I implore you by God's mercy to offer your very selves to him: a living sacrifice, dedicated and fit for his acceptance, the worship offered by mind and heart. Adapt yourselves no longer to the pattern of this present world, but let your minds be re-made, and your whole nature thus transformed. Then you will be able to discern the will of God, and to know what is good, acceptable and perfect. In virtue of the gift that God in his grace has given me, I say to everyone among you: Do not be conceited or think too highly of yourself; but think your way to a sober estimate based on the measure of faith that God has dealt to each of you. For just as in a single human body there are many limbs and organs, all with different functions, so all of us, united with Christ, form one body, serving individually as limbs and organs to each other.'

Once again in Philippians 4.18, the gifts which the Philippians have sent to him by Epaphroditus are described as 'a fragrant offering, an acceptable sacrifice, pleasing to God'. Their alms can be called 'sacrifice' because of the God-ward oblation of their whole lives.

Finally, there is Hebrews 13.10–17, a paragraph which begins with the words, 'Our altar is one from which the priests of the sacred tent have no right to eat'; and this ought surely to be taken as a direct reference to the Christian Eucharist, for this is the thing of which non-Christian Jews cannot partake. Needless to say, the 'altar' is not the Table used in the rite, for this use of the word does not begin till several centuries later: the word is used metaphorically, of the unseen reality of the Sacrifice of which the Eucharist is the outward and visible sacrament. In vv. 11–14 he speaks of the Jewish ritual in which the bodies of the victims are buried 'outside the camp', as a type of the crucifixion of Jesus outside the city gate, and calls on the Christians to 'go to him outside the camp, outside Judaism, 'bearing the stigma that he bore'. Then in v. 15 he says, 'Through Jesus, then let us continually offer up to God the sacrifice of praise, that is, the fruit of lips which acknowledge his name.' The word 'continually' refers to the confession of faith made in the whole of the daily life: and he continues, 'Never forget to show kindness and to share what you have with others; for such are the sacrifices which God approves.'

Thus, if we take this paragraph as a whole, it begins with the liturgical enactment of the Sacrifice of Christ in the Eucharist. Then it speaks of Christ's own sacrifice, consummated on the cross, and relates this to the duty of the readers in their present situation. It ends with the expression of the Universal Priesthood of all Christians in a daily life which is wholly a sacrificial life, directed Godwards, and finding expression in continual recollection of God's presence, in praise offered to him, and in acts of generosity and love towards men. The worship of God does not end when the liturgy is over: as in the Latin *Ite missa est*, the Church is dismissed from serving God in the liturgy to go out and serve him in his world.

CHAPTER VII

Sacrifice and Eucharist

(i) One Sacrifice and Many Eucharists

The basic affirmation of Christian faith is that God raised Jesus Christ from the dead. This is the same thing as to say, in sacrificial language, that his sacrifice is the *Accepted Sacrifice*; he is the Lamb of God, once offered in sacrifice, who takes away the sin of the world; his is the one, full, perfect and sufficient sacrifice for the sin of the whole world. But the Eucharist is a sacrificial action; his words at the Last Supper are in sacrificial language. What, then, is the relation between the One Sacrifice and the many Eucharists celebrated in many places all over the world, and at many times through the Christian centuries? We shall see how, especially in the middle ages in the West, the problem has been tangled up; and while the Reformation asserted some right principles, it was not able to give them adequate expression. Yet in our day fresh light on the problem seems to be coming.

Before we start on our study, it will be well to set out some important points, so that we may not have to digress from our study to discuss them.

(a) *The Old Testament* is fulfilled in the New. But at certain points there has been a tendency to neglect this principle of Fulfilment. Both Priesthood and Sacrifice have often been construed along Old Testament lines, as when in Hippolytus we find the bishop spoken of as a 'high-priest', without any attempt to relate this to the High-priesthood of Christ, and in the use of the word 'propitiation'.

In pagan religion generally, sacrifice could be offered to neutralize some malign influence, or avert the wrath of some deity; this can be illustrated from a few places in the Old Testament, such as 2 Kings 3.27, where such practice is described. But the biblical writers themselves have to wrestle with this problem as it concerns the wrath of the God of Israel. In seeking the answer, they see him sometimes as the One who makes propitiation and actively shows mercy, rather than as the One who is propitiated.[1] But it is not till the New Testament that the answer comes out fully clear: 'Herein is love, not that we loved God but that he loved us, and sent his Son, to be the propitiation for our sins' (1 John 4.10, R.V.) or, 'as the remedy for defilement of our sins' (N.E.B.).

The wrath of God is real indeed. But God hates only hatred; therefore he must judge in wrath hard-hearted egoistic man whose mind is centred on the self. He does not hate sinners, for he sent his Son to be the propitiation for their sins, by cleansing them from their defilement. The new Dominican paper-back edition of the Psalter[2] appends to each psalm a Prayer suggesting the Christian interpretation of it. In the case of Psalm 109 (108) this Prayer is:

Lord Jesus Christ, who didst pray for thy executioners,
  'Father, forgive them for they know not what they do,'
Thou didst bless when men cursed thee:
Teach us to hate only hatred and to curse only evil itself.
  That God may forgive us our offences,
    as we forgive those who have offended against us,
    and may be delivered at the last from the judgement of the Curse.

(b) How do we interpret the word '*anamnesis*' in the words 'Do this in remembrance of me'? Is each Eucharist a 'memorial-

---

[1] See my article on the word 'Atone' in the *Theological Word-book of the Bible*, ed. A. Richardson, pp. 25–6.

[2] *Le Psautier de la Bible de Jérusalem.* Les Editions du Cerf, Paris (1961), pp. 253–5.

Sacrifice and Eucharist

sacrifice' (Hebrew *zikkaron*, Greek *mnemosynon*) before God? But *anamnesis* and the corresponding verb are in the Septuagint the rendering of '*azkarah*', which means 'a remembering'.[1] And the Hebrew mind does not understand the word 'to remember' in the subjective and psychological sense which is habitual to us, but in an active sense. When the Lord 'remembers' Hannah in 1 Samuel 1.19–20 she has a baby; when he 'remembers his mercy' he 'helps his servant Israel' (Luke 1.54, the *Magnificat*); when he 'remembers' our sins, he chastises us. In these ways his Righteousness manifests itself as active and operative, in mercy or in judgement.

So it is in two specially interesting passages: 1 Kings 17.18, and Numbers 5.15. In the former passage, Elijah is lodging with the widow of Zarephath, and after a while her child dies. Then she says to him, 'What have you against me, O man of God? You have come to me to bring my sin to remembrance, and to cause the death of my son!' Yet Elijah has not said a word about her sins. The thought is, that the presence of the holy man in the house has set in motion hidden spiritual forces, and the woman's past sins which had been covered (as it were) with a layer of dust, are now exposed, and (as it were) come to life, and destroy the life of the little boy. It is the same in Numbers 5, which describes a dreadful trial by ordeal, in a case where a husband is convinced that his wife has committed adultery but has no direct evidence (vv. 12–14). There is to be a sacrifice which is described in detail in vv. 15–28; *if* the woman is innocent, nothing is to happen; but *if* she is guilty, the curse is to come upon her and 'her body swell and her thigh

---

[1] There is one instance in the LXX where *anamnesis* is used to denote an 'act of memorial before God': it is Lev. 24.7, the passage about the Shewbread. There are the twelve cakes of shewbread, arranged in two rows (vv. 5–6): then 'thou shalt put pure frankincense upon each row, that it may be to the bread for a memorial, even an offering made by fire unto the LORD' (v. 7). But the LXX mistranslates this as, 'they (the cakes) shall serve for a memorial'—but here the word could not be *mnemosynon*, for the cakes were not burnt. So the best that the translator could now do was to write *eis anamnesin*, and omit altogether the clause about the offering made by fire. So W. M. F. Scott, 'The Eucharist and the Heavenly Ministry of our Lord' in *Theology*, Feb. 1953, p. 43.

fall away'. For this is a sacrifice 'of remembrance, bringing iniquity to remembrance,' if there is iniquity there.

In these two instances, guilty sin is thought of as 'brought to remembrance', so that it takes deadly effect. But when our Lord says 'Do this in remembrance of me' or 'for my memorial', that which is brought back out of the past into the present to become active and operative here and now, is his Sacrifice, his body given and his blood shed, for the bringing in of the New Covenant of God with man. The One Sacrifice is 'made-present', that it may have its effect in the cleansing and healing of the Covenant-people.[1]

(c) There is also *man's part*. Even when we are saved and justi-fied only by God's saving mercy, our part is not merely passive. When God carries out for us men the whole work of our salvation, he still treats us as personal beings, and demands of us our all in return.[2] Liberated by Grace, man is set free to act with all his might, in serving God with mind, heart and will. In the Euchar-ist he thanks God, making remembrance of what he must thank God for, and he makes petitions, through Jesus Christ his Lord, desiring that the petitions may be according to the mind of Christ and may be united with his heavenly intercession. All this is the work of the Holy Spirit in man; 'we do not even know how we ought to pray, but through our inarticulate groans the Spirit himself is pleading for us' (Romans 8.26). Through the Spirit, man prays as a member of Christ's body. And as the Eucharist is a sacrificial action, in it man offers sacrifice. The sense in which he offers sacrifice must be deter-mined by the Christian meaning of sacrifice, as the New Testa-ment sets it forth. How has this been interpreted in the Church?

(ii) *Eucharistic Sacrifice, down to the Middle Ages*

The patristic period, which can be reckoned as lasting in the

[1] For all this, see my article in the *Theological Word-book of the Bible*, s.v. 'Memory', pp. 142–3. Also Gregory Dix in *The Parish Communion*, pp. 120–1. To him I myself owe this interpretation of 'memory'.

[2] See Prof. Moule's paper on 'The Sacrifice of the People of God' in *The Parish Communion Today*, pp. 83–93.

Sacrifice and Eucharist

West until the Roman Empire was swamped by the barbarian invasions, was the great creative period in Christian theology, when the doctrines of the Trinity and the Incarnation were worked out. It was also the great creative period in Liturgy, for by the sixth century the great liturgies of the East and the West had received their classical shape. Both in faith and in worship there was a Truth by which the Church lived, and which it knew in its inner consciousness; and this was prior to the intellectual formulations of it. So it was that in this period the Church was living by the eucharistic sacrifice, and yet even a bold pioneer such as St. Cyril of Jerusalem could do no more than throw out suggestions towards the theological formulation of it. The reality itself was known by the Church most typically in the Easter Rite. Here there was the symbolism of the New fire and of Christ the Light of the World, and then after a long series of Scripture-lessons and chants, the preparation of the baptismal water for the baptism of a whole year's intake of converts; and after this they with the assembled Church did the action which was the Memorial of the Lord's Accepted Sacrifice, the reality which underlay their own death to sin and their share in his risen life. In the liturgical action, Professor (later Archbishop) Brilioth marked five 'aspects': Eucharistic Thanksgiving—Communion-fellowship—the historical Commemoration of the saving Events—the sacrificial Memorial—and the Mystery of the Lord's real presence in the here-and-now. They are not arranged in the right order; but taken together they give the idea of a wholeness and balance which in spite of all faults was on the whole everywhere kept through the patristic period.[1]

But a great change came, in the five centuries between St. Gregory the Great and the beginning of scholasticism, between 600 and 1100. As Dom Godfrey Diekmann, O.S.B., says:[2]

'This discovery is a relatively recent one. A current standard

[1] Yngve Brilioth, *Eucharistic Faith and Practice, Evangelical and Catholic*. E.T., S.P.C.K., London (1930).

[2] Diekmann, *Come, let us worship*, published in England by Darton, Longman and Todd (1962), pp. 8–9 and the rest of the chapter. Dom Diekmann is the editor of the American periodical *Worship*.

Down to the Middle Ages

reference has been, for instance, the four-volume work of Pourrat on *Christian Spirituality*. Now it is significant that Pourrat devotes the first volume to the era of the Fathers, i.e. to the first 600 years: then he begins the second volume (after a short, five-page nod to Cluny) with Saint Bernard, five centuries after the era of the Fathers, thus covering those five centuries in five pages! And yet in the two thousand years of the Church's existence, there has never been a more momentous change of outlook and practice in Christian spirituality than in these five centuries.'

In the rest of his first chapter he develops this theme, much as we have done in our Chapter V; the loss by the people of their share in the action, the evil effects of the anti-Arian struggle, the thought of Christ as above all the Divine Consecrator, the clericalization of the Mass.

We come then to St. Thomas Aquinas, who in the *Summa Theologica* devotes ten *quaestiones* mainly to the Real Presence and Transubstantiation, and only one to Eucharistic Sacrifice,[1] where he says that 'the celebration of this sacrament is a sort of image of Christ's passion' and also that 'since by it we are made partakers of the fruits of the Lord's passion, it is fittingly called the sacrifice (*immolatio*) of Christ' (*Summa*, III, 83.1). But he did also, elsewhere, give a definition of sacrifice as 'something done to things offered to God, as when animals were killed, and bread broken, eaten and blessed'. This is implied in the word itself, for *sacrificium* means that a man *facit aliquid sacrum* ('makes something, does something, holy')—*Summa*, IIa, IIae, 85, 3 ad 3. In another place he introduces the idea of propitiation: 'Sacrifice properly means something done to the honour of God, as is properly owed to him, to propitiate him (or, to appease him—*ad eum placandum*)'—*Summa*, III, 48.3. Is not sacrifice here being interpreted on the basis of classical and Old Testament usage, without any special regard to its New Testament meaning?[2]

---

[1] *Summa Theologica*, III, *quaestiones* 73–82 and 83 respectively.
[2] See for this B. J. Kidd, *The Later Mediaeval Doctrine of the Eucharistic Sacrifice*. S.P.C.K. (1898), pp. 49–57.

Sacrifice and Eucharist

Dr. Kidd quotes another dictum of St. Thomas, which became traditional and exercised much influence later on: 'The Eucharist is not only a sacrament, but also a sacrifice. . . . As a sacrifice, it has effect also on others for whom it is offered, in whom spiritual life may exist only in potentiality. So, if it finds right dispositions in them, it obtains grace for them by virtue of that Sacrifice from which all grace is derived for us; and it takes away mortal sins in them, not as the immediate cause, but by obtaining for them the grace of contrition. If it is objected that the Eucharist is offered only for those who are members of Christ, it can be replied that it is offered for members of Christ when it is offered for particular persons in order that they may become members.'[1] This is, as Kidd says, right enough in itself; but in the religious practice of the later Middle Ages it could be used to support a system in which the Mass, regarded as a propitiatory sacrifice, could be repeated again and again for particular intentions and was regarded as taking effect mechanically, *ex opere operato*, at the will of the priest.

So it came about that Pope Eugenius IV could affirm in the middle of the fifteenth century that the essential form for the ordination of a presbyter was the delivery to the ordinand of the chalice with wine and the paten with bread, and the words 'Receive the power of offering sacrifice in the Church for the living and the dead; in the name of the Father and of the Son and of the Holy Ghost.'[2] It was specially easy for new ceremonies to be introduced at Ordinations. In such a rite, it is natural for the person to be vested in the garments proper to his office (stole, chasuble, etc.), and to be given the things which he will use in the discharge of his office (Bible, chalice and paten, etc.); and as before the invention of printing, each bishop would have his own manuscript Ordinal—for he alone could use it—it was easy for new illustrative ceremonies to be added, and then for them to be imitated by other bishops.[3]

---

[1] Quoted in Kidd, op. cit., pp. 54–5. The translation is mine.
[2] W. K. Firminger in *Liturgy and Worship*. Ed. Clarke, S.P.C.K. (1932), pp. 643, 657.
[3] ibid., p. 655.

Such a ceremony was the anointing of the new priest's hands; it was beautiful and appropriate, and was widely adopted. But the next thing was that it became a widespread opinion in the period before St. Thomas that the anointing of the hands was the essential matter of the Sacrament of Orders.[1] So it was with the delivery of the chalice and paten, with the accompanying words; when it had become habitual, its recent origin was forgotten, and it became the official view.

The seriousness of this is expressed in some words of Gregory Dix, the reference of which in the original context is to the stipendiary masses. He wrote that there came to be

'a practical divorce of those complementary ideas of the corporate offering and the priesthood of the priest, whose combination is essential to any organic doctrine of the Church as well as of the Eucharist. Without it, the Eucharist is turned into something which a priest alone can do simply in virtue of his personal possession of holy orders, without due regard being had to the fact that the Eucharist is the corporate act of the Church.'[2]

So it came about that things happened which in our day would appear in newspaper headlines such as 'Ten thousand Masses for the repose of the soul of King Henry V'.

(iii) *Eucharist and Sacrifice in the Reformation*

Luther, as we have said, totally rejected the current idea of the 'Sacrifices of Masses'. He rejected the whole false religious practice which had turned the sacrament of God's redeeming Grace into a 'work' performed by men to propitiate his wrath. He wrote in *The Babylonian Captivity of the Church* (1520), when he himself was still celebrating according to the old rite:

'Let the priests who offer the sacrifice of the mass in these corrupt and most perilous times take care, firstly, that the words of the greater and lesser canons of the mass [i.e. the canon proper, and the offertory prayers, respectively], to-

---

[1] ibid., pp. 658–9.
[2] Dix, *The Shape of the Liturgy*, p. 594.

gether with all the collects which all too plainly re-echo the sense of sacrifice, do not refer to the sacrament, but either just to the bread and wine, which the Words consecrate, or to their own prayers. Indeed, the bread and wine were formerly offered in order to receive the blessing, and so become sanctified by the word and by prayers. After the blessing and consecration, they are no longer offerings, but gifts received from God.'[1]

Throughout his life, and not only in his conflict with Zwingli, Luther contended for the real presence of the Lord in the consecrated elements. In 1545, a few months before his death, one Adam Besserer had delivered to a communicant an unconsecrated Bread, as the breads on the paten had fallen on the ground. Luther's friend Amsdorf had censured him severely for this and had even had him put in prison; whereupon Luther wrote to him on 11th January 1546: 'Yes, this is no matter of indifference; it is a grave fault, a very grave fault, on the part of this priest. . . . He must not be allowed to minister to our congregations; let him go off to his Zwinglians! It is not necessary to keep such a man in prison.'[2]

Zwingli and also some of Luther's followers such as Carlstadt, whom Luther disowned as 'fanatics', held that the Memorial-act was simply a human commemoration of a past event. This rationalism has repeatedly found expression since then, and has appeared among Liberal Protestants in our own time. Yet it is really basic to Christian faith and devotion that the holy sacrament be confessed to be a supernatural reality, a Mystery, a real presence of the risen and ascended Lord with his people; and orthodox Protestantism has always held to this. So for instance the Scots' Confession of 1560 affirms:

'We utterly damne the vanity of thay that affirme Sacramentes to be nothing ellis but naked and baire signes.'

Calvin, who uses all his logical acuteness to criticize at great length any idea of a local presence in the elements, since the

[1] *Reformation Writings of Martin Luther.* E.T., Lee-Wolff, Vol. I, p. 251; quoted by Bro. George Every in *The Parish Communion Today*, p. 98.
[2] R. Prenter, *Reformatoren Martin Luther*, p. 43.

natural body of Christ is in heaven and not here, stops all of a sudden to confess in a wonderful passage that there is a mystery here which passes human understanding:

'Now, should anyone ask me as to the mode (of the presence) I will not be ashamed to confess that it is too high a mystery either for my mind to comprehend or my words to express; and to speak more plainly, I rather feel than understand it. The truth of God therefore in which I can safely rest, I embrace without controversy. He declares that his flesh is the meat, his blood the drink, of my soul; I give my soul to him to be fed with such food. In his sacred Supper he bids me take, eat and drink his body and blood under the symbols of bread and wine. I have no doubt that he will truly give and I receive.'[1]

Coming now to the Church of England, we must cite first Article XXXI, *of the one oblation of Christ finished upon the Cross:*

The offering of Christ once made, is the perfect redemption, propitiation and satisfaction for all the sins of the whole world, both original and actual, and there is none other satisfaction for sin, but that alone. Wherefore the sacrifices of Masses, in the which it was commonly said that the priest(s) did offer Christ for the quick and the dead, to have remission of pain or guilt, were blasphemous fables, and dangerous deceits.

This is the text of 1571, previous versions having appeared in 1553 and 1563, and the canons of Trent 'On the sacrifice of the mass' having been promulgated in September 1562.[2] It is to be remembered that the men who compiled the Article had all seen the liturgical changes that had taken place in England, and had known the practice which had previously existed. The second sentence of the Article condemns (i) not 'the sacrifice of the Mass' but 'the sacrifices of Masses', as in the chantry chapels; (ii) the belief that the priests (not as in 1553 'the

---

[1] Calvin, *Institutes of the Christian Religion*, IV, xvii, 32. E.T. by Beveridge, Vol. II, p. 587.

[2] B. J. Kidd, *The Later Mediaeval Doctrine of the Eucharistic Sacrifice*. S.P.C.K. (1898), pp. 6–10.

priest') offered Christ for the living and for the souls in Purgatory. Such propitiatory sacrifices were a practical denial of the One Sacrifice, affirmed in the first sentence of the Article; hence the word 'Wherefore' in the second. (iii) What is condemned is the current belief; hence the words 'it was commonly said'. There is therefore here no denial of any and every belief that the Mass is a sacrificial action. The compilers of the Article were in the midst of the controversy, and knew also what Trent had said; they weighed their words, and knew exactly what they meant to say.[1]

We turn next, therefore, to the rites of 1549 and 1552, to examine just what it is that the priest and people are said to do and to 'offer' in these two rites. For the two rites are substantially the same in this respect. The Act of Uniformity to which the Book of 1552 was attached spoke of the 1549 Book as 'a very godly order . . . agreeable to the Word of God and the primitive Church, very comfortable to all good people desiring to live in Christian conversation, and most profitable to the state of this Realm;' while the new Book was said to be 'for the more plain

---

[1] Kidd, op. cit., pp. 10–24, and the rest of the chapter. But any discussion of Article XXXI must now take into account the competent, learned and fully-documented work of Fr. Francis Clark, S.J., *Eucharistic Sacrifice and the Reformation* (Darton, Longman and Todd, 1960), who criticizes Dr. Kidd's book and the many Anglican writers who have been influenced by it. He readily admits, of course, that there were in the late middle ages manifold abuses and superstitions, but insists that the Church's eucharistic teaching was basically sound. When, however, he states for himself the 'Catholic' doctrine with which he is working, as he does many times, it is that 'the Christian priesthood is essentially ordained to bring about the real presence of Christ by the Eucharistic consecration and to offer him thus objectively present in a propitiatory sacrifice for the living and the dead' (p. 191). Here the share of the assembled Church in the sacrificial action is not mentioned, and the whole emphasis is on the priest's offering to God of the consecrated elements. The picture in mind is not that of the local Church-community with communion of the people, but rather of the priest at some side-altar saying his mass. Was it not just this that our forefathers most radically objected to, though it was difficult for them at that time to define in precise terms what their real objection was? and is it not this that most of the Anglican writers whom he quotes are trying to escape from, while affirming the reality of the sacrificial action? As for Dr. Kidd, it seems to me that my own citations from him are all valid.

and manifest explanation hereof' and 'for the more perfection of the said order of Common prayer'.[1] In 1552, Cranmer was under extreme pressure from the Swiss Reformers; but an examination of the words 'offer' and 'sacrifice' will show that in this respect he was not going back on the rite of 1549. We will confine our comments to this point, and not describe the many differences between the two rites.

(a) There is the offering of the bread and wine, which in the rubrics at the end of the 1549 rite are offerings of the people, provided by different families in turn, but in 1552 are not mentioned at all. Yet there must have been bread and wine placed on the Holy Table, or the rite could not proceed; and it may have been the intention of the compilers of 1552 that the bread and wine should be placed on the Table immediately before the *sursum corda*.[2]

(b) In both rites it is emphasized in the strongest terms in the Prayer which in 1662 was entitled 'the Prayer of Consecration', that our Lord's Sacrifice is 'one, full, perfect and sufficient'; and then it is said that he instituted and commanded us to continue 'a perpetual memory of that his precious death, until his coming again'. In both books, then, this is what is being done in the rite; and in 1549 it is stated immediately after the Words of Institution, that we having in remembrance his death and passion and resurrection, and ascension, 'do celebrate and make here before thy divine Majesty, with these thy holy gifts, the memorial which thy Son hath willed us to make'. Thus the action of the Eucharist is defined in terms of our Lord's institution. The word 'memorial' or 'memory' has been discussed earlier in this chapter; it is not a sacrifice offered to call God to mind, but a remembering which is a bringing-back-out-of-the-past-into-the-present of the sacrifice of Christ, so that it is here and now operative in its effects. Its effects are the cleansing and healing of mankind, which are mediated in the sacrament.

(c) For both in 1549 and in 1552 we have the prayer to God

[1] Brightman, *The English Rite*, Vol. I, pp. 9 and 19. Cf. also Humphrey Whitby, *The End of Sacrifice*. S.P.C.K. (1942), pp. 7 ff.
[2] So Whitby argues, in *The End of Sacrifice*, pp. 27–8.

'to accept this our sacrifice of praise and thanksgiving'; and by this phrase Cranmer certainly meant, as his controversy with Gardiner shows, not 'a sacrifice propitiatory' but 'a sacrifice gratificatory', an act of thanksgiving for the One Accepted Sacrifice.[1] Such a sacrifice is laid before him in the memorial-action, with the petition that as Christ's own Sacrifice is universal, so its effects may be universal, and 'we and all thy whole Church may obtain remission of our sins and all other benefits of his passion'.

(d) It proceeds: 'And here we offer and present unto thee ourselves, our souls and bodies' to be a reasonable, holy and lively sacrifice into thee; this being involved in our union with the Lord in Holy Communion. We express thus our will to offer ourselves; but knowing our frailty, we have to add the petition 'that all we who are partakers of this Holy Communion may be fulfilled with thy grace and heavenly benediction'. 1549 is fuller here, speaking of the communicants' union with the Lord as members of his body, 'that he may dwell in them and they in him'.

(e) Finally, we sinners who are not worthy to offer to him any sacrifice, pray him 'to accept this our bounden duty and service'—i.e. plainly, the liturgical action which we have performed in obedience to our Lord's command—'not weighing our merits but pardoning our offences, through Jesus Christ our Lord, by whom and with whom, in the unity of the Holy

---

[1] Cranmer's words are: 'To defend the papistical error that the daily offering of the priest in the Mass is propitiatory, you extend the word "propitiation" otherwise than the apostles do. I speak plainly, according to St. Paul and St. John, that only Christ is the propitiation for our sins by his death. You speak according to the papists, that the priests in their masses make a sacrifice propitiatory. I call a sacrifice propitiatory, according to the Scripture, such a sacrifice as pacifieth God's indignation against us, obtaineth mercy and forgiveness of all our sins, and is our ransom and redemption from eternal damnation. And on the other side, I call a sacrifice gratificatory, or the sacrifice of the Church, such a sacrifice as doth not reconcile us to God, but is made of (by) them that be reconciled, to testify their duties and to show themselves thankful unto him. And these sacrifices in Scripture be not called propitiatory, but sacrifices of justice, of laud, praise and thanksgiving.'—*Cranmer's Works.* Parker Society, p. 371; quoted by Kidd, op. cit., pp. 27–8.

Ghost, all honour and glory be unto thee, O Father Almighty, world without end. Amen.' For through Jesus the Lord the worship of the whole redeemed creation returns to its Creator.

In this there is one consistent idea. Our action in the Eucharist is a sacrificial action, in the sense in which the New Testament interprets the idea of sacrifice; yet it is not an additional sacrifice to the Accepted Sacrifice of our Saviour, but falls wholly within the scope of that One Sacrifice. It is wrong, therefore, to interpret the Prayer Book rite in the sense that the only 'sacrifice' in it is the oblation of ourselves, our souls and bodies.

The central point in this exposition is the interpretation of 'our sacrifice of praise and thanksgiving'. But here also is the problem; for there are many among us Anglicans who are sure that the Eucharist is an act of sacrifice, but see no way to express this except that which seems to be implied in the Roman Canon: 'We offer to thy glorious Majesty, of thy gifts to us, a pure Host (*hostia*, victim), a holy Host, a spotless Host, the holy Bread of eternal life and the Cup of everlasting salvation.' Hence the words 'our sacrifice of praise and thanksgiving' are taken to mean an offering of the consecrated elements to God; and in some of the revisions in the Anglican Provinces overseas words are added such as 'we offer to thee the Bread of eternal life and the Cup of everlasting salvation'. So in some of our hymns we speak of 'pleading the sacrifice of Christ'.

But can it be right to plead with God to accept the One Sacrifice of his Son, which he has once for all accepted when he raised him from the dead? Max Thurian places at the beginning of his book *L'Eucharistie* the words of Du Moulin (1635): 'Il se peut dire qu'en la Sainte Cène nous offrons Jesus-Christ à Dieu, en tant que nous prions Dieu qu'il reçoive pour nous le sacrifice de sa mort.'[1] Can this be right?

It can indeed be rightly said that in the Eucharist above all the Church prays to God 'through Jesus Christ our Lord', and

[1] 'It can be said that in the Holy Supper we offer Jesus Christ to God, since there we pray God to accept on our behalf the Sacrifice of his death.' The book is *L'Eucharistie*, by Max Thurian, Frère de Taizé, printed at Taizé and published by Delachaux et Niestlé, Neuchâtel and Paris.

Sacrifice and Eucharist

we seek to unite our offering and our prayer with his intercession for us, as being members of his body. What are we to say here? for we are in deep waters; we are speaking of great things. We can certainly pray, *unconditionally*, that Christ's purpose in the redemption of mankind may be fulfilled, so that 'we and all his whole Church may obtain . . . all the benefits of his passion'. But does this apply to temporal requests, and to the offering of the Eucharist for particular intentions? It is right for us, of course, to bring to God particular subjects of prayer; for as the Intention of Christ's own Sacrifice is universal, so the intention of every Eucharist is really universal, though we in our frailty can only think of one thing at a time. But particular and temporary petitions cannot be offered unconditionally. In Gethsemane he himself could not pray 'Abba, Father, all things are possible to thee; take this cup away from me', without adding immediately, 'Yet not what I will, but what thou wilt'. This sets the universal rule for our particular and temporal petitions; they can only be made *conditionally*, 'if it is thy will'. We cannot plead the Sacrifice of Christ in the Eucharist as a sure means of obtaining what we desire from God, thinking that we can 'placate' God or 'propitiate' him by pleading the Sacrifice of his Son. We are indeed to offer, and we are to bring our petitions and present our needs. But there is peril in the idea that the Eucharist can be offered for particular intentions; the peril is that our act of offering may be put by us on a sub-Christian level.

As for the words quoted from the Latin canon, the earliest form in which they occur is that of Hippolytus, 'We offer to thee the bread and the cup, giving thanks to thee that thou hast allowed us to stand before thee and perform our priestly ministry'. This means that the offertory-action of offering to God the bread and wine in their natural substances continues throughout the Eucharistic Prayer;[1] and this can have been the meaning of the words quoted from the Canon, in their earlier forms.[2]

[1] Gregory Dix in *The Parish Communion*. ed. Hebert, 1937, p. 112.
[2] See Bro. George Every in *The Parish Communion Today*, pp. 99–100 and 103–4.

Since the Counter-Reformation

(iv) *Roman Catholic Teaching since the Counter-Reformation*

After the breach with the Protestants had taken place, the Roman Church had to make its reply at the Council of Trent to Luther's criticisms of the current doctrine and practice.[1] There was now a controversial need to uphold the Church's practice, while at the same time some notice must be taken of the Protestant criticisms. We can here only summarize the matter in the briefest way. The criticism expressed—for instance in the Anglican Article XXXI, was met by affirming the truth of the One Sacrifice, and that the Mass is the representation and 'memory' of that Sacrifice (Session xxii, Ch. 1), and that it is a sacrifice offered by him, but now in an 'un-bloody' manner, and as such is 'truly propitiatory' (ibid., Ch. 2). The Canons, however, are more trenchant, and pronounce anathemas on all who say that 'a true and proper sacrifice is not offered to God in the Mass' (Canon I), or that 'the Sacrifice of the Mass is only a sacrifice of praise and thanksgiving', or 'a bare commemoration of the Sacrifice of the Cross, and not propitiatory', or 'is of benefit to the communicant only'; or 'that it ought not to be offered for the living and the dead for sins, penalties, satisfactions and other needs' (Canon III). Here Anglicans, Zwinglians and Lutherans are condemned in turn, and the current Roman Catholic practice upheld.

The theologians of this and the following period in the Roman Church were seeking for some way of envisaging the sacrificial action in the Mass as a re-enacting of the immolation of Christ once for all on the Cross.[2] Thus for Melchior Cano, the fraction of the host re-enacts the 'breaking' of his body. Salmeron, Vasquez and Lessius see the separate consecration of the bread and wine as a symbol of the separation of his body and blood in death. De Lugo and Franzelin see in the tran-

---

[1] The whole subject is treated with some fullness in B. J. Kidd, *The Later Mediaeval Doctrine of the Eucharistic Sacrifice*, pp. 58 to the end of the book. On the Council of Trent, pp. 115–20. Like most Anglicans of that day— and this is a very early work of Dr. Kidd—he is quite unfair to Luther.

[2] A good and widely read account of this subject is given by Dr. E. L. Mascall, in his book *Corpus Christi*. Longmans (1953), Ch. IV.

Sacrifice and Eucharist

substantiation itself a kind of *kenosis*, a self-emptying or humiliation of the Christ who is now glorified, yet condescends to be present with us and be offered by us in this lowly form.

But in recent Roman Catholic theology there has been a most remarkable re-interpretation of the Sacrifice of the Mass, in a way which Protestants will no longer feel obliged to reject. Thus Canon Masure criticizes trenchantly the Counter-Reformation teaching of a sacrifice in the Mass consisting of a destruction of the divine victim, as when de Lugo said that 'there is a death on the corporal' and there Christ is 'continually dying to make intercession for us' (*semper moriens ad interpellandum pro nobis*).[1]

Fr. de la Taille, S.J., in his great book *Mysterium Fidei* (1915) rejected the idea that each Mass is a fresh *immolation* of Christ; for he cannot die again. Rather, each Mass is a fresh *oblation* of Christ, after his death and resurrection, just as the Last Supper was such an oblation in the night before he suffered. The Mass is then no repetition of Calvary; rather it interprets his death as the One Sacrifice, as he himself did at the Last Supper. Sir William Spens popularized this view for us Anglicans: 'The Last Supper and the Eucharist are not separate sacrifices from that of Calvary, but supply a necessary element in the sacrifice of Calvary, by expressly investing our Lord's death, before God and men, with its sacrificial significance.[2]

Such Roman Catholic teaching as that of de la Taille we can not only not reject, but acclaim with joy. The same applies to the teaching of Abbot Anscar Vonier, in his *Key to the Doctrine of the Holy Eucharist* (1925). Here the key-word is 'Sacrament': the Eucharist is a sacramental sign which not only represents the thing signified, but re-presents it, makes it present, an efficacious sign. The sacramental presence in the Mass is real, but is different from his presence in bodily form on earth during his ministry, and from the presence in heaven of the Ascended One; and it exists because by his institution and promise he has attached it to certain outward and visible signs. Hence, in

---

[1] E. Masure, *Le Sacrifice du Chef* (E.T. *The Christian Sacrifice*, p. 223).
[2] Sir William Spens in *Essays Catholic and Critical* (1925), p. 436.

Mascall's words, 'it is not a repetition of the Sacrifice, nor is it the completion of the Sacrifice; it is simply the Sacrifice itself, present in the unique mode of a Sacrament; present, that is, simply and solely because the consecrated species are the divinely ordained effective signs of it. The inner reality which the Sacramental Signs contain—namely, the whole redemptive act of Christ—does not *happen* historically and physically, in the Mass: it is simply *there*, sacramentally. As something done by the Church, as the saying of certain words and the doing of certain things with the sacramental species, each Mass is of course a new event: but it is not a new event in the life of Christ.'[1]

Canon Masure's book, *The Christian Sacrifice*,[2] is truly magisterial. He thinks of Sacrifice as summing up the whole God-ward movement of man; and so, before he comes to treat of eucharistic sacrifice, he goes to the gospels and treats of the whole story of God made man, of the true Godhead of the Son and his true manhood, and of his sacrifice as the consummation of his work in a world of sin. Like Vonier, he dwells on the Sacrament or Sign of his sacrifice which he gave us at the Last Supper, and sees the Mass as the Church's act of sacrifice, summing up the wholeness of the mysteries of creation and redemption and the Church's life in Christ. It is a book to delight Protestants as well as Catholics, because of its firm Scriptural foundation.

Another liturgical theologian has been Dom Odo Casel, of Maria Laach Abbey in the Rhineland, who has interpreted the *anamnesis* as the *Gegenwärtigsetzung* or 'making present' of the work of redemption once for all accomplished in Jesus Christ, so that in the holy sacrament it becomes here and now present and active and operative. This thought is expressed in the 'secret' for the ninth Sunday after Pentecost in the Roman rite: *quoties hujus hostiae commemoratio celebratur, opus nostrae redemptionis exercetur*—'every time that the memorial of this saving Victim is celebrated, the work of our redemption is set in movement'.

[1] E. L. Mascall, *Corpus Christi*, p. 96.
[2] E. Masure, *Le Sacrifice du Chef*; E.T. *The Christian Sacrifice*, by Dom Illtyd Trethowan, of Downside. Burns and Oates (1944).

Sacrifice and Eucharist

In face of such eucharistic teaching by responsible Roman Catholic theologians, which is spreading more and more widely in the Roman Church, Protestants will surely find that most of their traditional objections are melting away, and that they themselves have much to learn. It is a very fresh wind that is blowing in the Roman Church today; and it may be that before very long it will be openly said that eucharistic sacrifice is no longer a subject of controversy between Protestants and Catholics, since both sides acknowledge the Sacrifice of Christ to be the One Accepted Sacrifice. This will be hastened, in proportion as both sides learn to listen to what Eastern Orthodoxy has to teach us.

(v) *Light from the East*

All through this book we have been so occupied with the tangled history of the West, that we have had scarcely anything to say about the Orthodox Eastern Churches. The West and the East have lived apart for centuries. But the Easterns, who have remained outside our controversies, have a disconcerting way of being more catholic than Western Catholics and more evangelical than Western Evangelicals. New Delhi, 1961, showed that the Eastern Christians intend to take a full share in ecumenical discussions.

Another thing that has largely been missing in this book, as in most Western theological books, is any serious treatment of the doctrine of the Holy Spirit. And this is something that the East understands more deeply than the West. It so happens that in the first number of *Studia Liturgica*, the new ecumenical Quarterly,[1] an article appears by Fr. Boris Bobrinskoy about 'the Holy Spirit in the Liturgy',[2] of which I will attempt to give some sort of an account.

[1] *Studia Liturgica* is edited by Pastor W. Vos, Mathenesserlaan 301C, Rotterdam, Holland, and is obtainable by subscription (fl. 13, post free) to Studia Liturgica, Postbus 2, Niewendam, Holland.

[2] 'Le Saint-Esprit dans la Liturgie' by Boris Bobrinskoy, priest of the Russian Orthodox Church, and a professor at the Institut Saint-Serge, the Orthodox Seminary in Paris.

Light from the East

The nature of the Holy Spirit is such that his presence and activity are peculiarly difficult to describe in our conceptual language. Yet the Church knows him. 'The world cannot receive him', says our Lord in John 14.17, 'because the world neither sees him nor knows him; but you know him, for he dwells with you and in you.' The fourteenth-century theologian Nicholas Cabasilas quotes these words, and continues: 'It is this Spirit who by the acts and words of the priests hallows the Holy Mysteries.' But our Lord is not content only to send the Holy Spirit to dwell with us, for he himself has promised to 'be with us always, to the end of time' (Matt. 28.20). The Paraclete is present invisibly, because he never takes to himself a body: but the Saviour, by means of the tremendous and sacred Mysteries, allows himself to be there seen and touched, because he has taken to himself our human nature, and retains it for ever' (p. 58).

The Eucharist, as Father Boulgakoff put it, is a *leiturgeia*, a work done in common. In the Orthodox rite, in which the prayers of the Minister and the faithful are united together and woven into one with one another, the sacrament is performed by the community, by all the people together with the Minister, and the power to perform the consecration or 'transformation' rests not in a quasi-magical act, *ex opere operato*, done apart from the people and without their co-operation (that is to say, apart from the Church), but as a liturgy, a work done in common (p. 51).

The consecratory *Epiclesis* is universal in the Eastern rites; it is found in the West in the ancient Mozarabic, Gallican and Celtic rites; it is found in the *Apostolic Tradition* of St. Hippolytus (in spite of the contrary view of Dom Gregory Dix); but it has been missing from the Roman rite from the early fifth century. 'We meet then with the strange phenomenon of a "regression" of the Epiclesis in the West, which coincides in time with the strong awareness which Eastern Christendom gained of the person and action of the Holy Spirit in the Church and specially in the Eucharist, an awareness specially clear in St. Cÿril of Jerusalem and St. Basil of Caesarea. Yet this "regression" at

Sacrifice and Eucharist

Rome is limited to the eucharistic canon, for an *epiclesis* occurs, preceded by *sursum corda*, etc. in the rites for the blessing of the chrism for confirmation, and of the baptismal water' (pp. 53–4).

As for the theology of the Epiclesis, there is nothing automatic or mechanical in the presence of Christ and of the Holy Spirit. It calls for the earnest supplications of the Church, of the whole People of God gathered for the eucharistic feast. All the eucharistic prayers including those which precede and those which follow the Canon have this character of Epiclesis or Invocation; the preceding prayers, that the Holy Spirit may enable us to call on the Father to consecrate the body and blood of Christ, and those which come after, that the Father will accept our sacrifice and pour out on the faithful the fullness of his Grace (p. 55).

The Words of Institution are not consecratory in the Orthodox view, as they are in the Roman Church, and in the teaching of St. Thomas Aquinas who held that they are consecratory when pronounced by a priest even outside their context in the liturgy. This is natural and logical for Latin theology, which holds that the Words of Institution are pronounced by the priest *in persona Christi*, the priest representing Christ. Such a definition of the priestly ministry is not acceptable to the Orthodox: for he who presides in the eucharistic assembly does not consecrate alone, *ex sese*, in the presence of a passive congregation; the Eucharist is 'liturgical', i.e. it is the common action of the whole assembled people, in whose name and with whom the Minister acts. It is the congregation which is the local embodiment of the Church, of the Church in all its fullness and catholicity, the Body of Christ and the Bride of Christ: that whole congregation which of all the members, both hierarchy and people, are united to Christ through the descent of the Holy Spirit, in the eucharistic act of Communion (pp. 55–6).

There is then a real presence of the Son by means of the Holy Spirit in the Eucharist, and no less a real presence of the Spirit through the Son. The Persons are not interchangeable; they are different. Just before the beginning of the eucharistic Canon come the words, 'The *grace* of our Lord Jesus Christ, the *love* of

Light from the East

God the Father, and the *communion* (sharing) of the Holy Spirit be with you all.' So in the Liturgy of St. Basil, just after the Epiclesis: 'and all us who partake of the one bread and the cup, do thou unite together in the communion of one Holy Spirit, and grant that no one among us may partake of the holy Body and holy Blood of thy Christ unto judgement and condemnation' (56–7).

What are we to say to all this? That the Orthodox in their liturgy know the Holy Spirit better than we; as in the text quoted earlier, 'You know him, because he dwells with you and in you.' It is not that the Easterns hold that the Epiclesis is the 'correct' method of consecration, as a Western liturgist might who wanted an Epiclesis to be added in some Western rite. They say rather that the Liturgy as a whole is an epiclesis, and the words of the Epiclesis thus form a focal point of the rite. They hold that in all rites, including the Roman, the elements are hallowed by prayer in the Spirit and not by the recitation of the Words of Institution; for while in the Roman canon the Spirit is not invoked in an Epiclesis, prayer is made again and again that the gifts may be accepted and blessed. This, say the Easterns, is the real form of consecration. So many Western theologians believed before the thirteenth century, and many so believe again today. The real difference between the East and the West is not about the form of consecration, but about the relation between the Consecration and the Sacrifice—whether they are one and the same, or the Sacrifice consists in an offering by the priest to God of the consecrated Gifts.[1]

[1] Cf. Bro. George Every, in *The Parish Communion Today*, pp. 96–100.

CHAPTER VIII

Ordained and Unordained Lay-men

★

The point of the title of this chapter[1] is that all Christians, clerical and lay alike, are members of the *Laos*, the People of God, and all alike share in the Priesthood of All Believers which is affirmed in Exodus 19.5–6 and 1 Peter 2.5 and 9,[2] and of which the sign and seal is the Sacrament of Baptism. This Universal Priesthood, which is a designation of the whole life and ministry of Christians in the Church, is never rightly understood and never becomes effectual in practice, unless there is a clear view of the authority and functions of the Ordained Ministry. Such is the thesis of this chapter.

We will begin with another Orthodox quotation, from Khomiakoff the great Russian theologian of the nineteenth century.

(i) *The Solidarity of the Body of Christ*

This title is an attempt to put into English what we call 'the Communion of Saints, or the Greek *koinonia* or the Russian *sobornost'*. Khomiakoff is speaking of the operation of the Holy Spirit in the People of God, particularly in the life of prayer:[3]

[1] I owe this title to the opening words of the report by Lt.-Col. Madge of one of the discussion groups at the 'Parish and People' Conference at Swanwick in January 1962.

[2] pp. 93–4 and 102–5 above.

[3] In *Birkbeck and the Russian Church*. Ed. Athelstan Riley, published by S.P.C.K., London (1917), pp. 349–53.

The Body of Christ

'We know that when anyone of us falls, he falls alone; but no one is saved alone. He who is saved is saved in the Church, as a member of her, and in unity with her other members. If anyone believes, he is in the communion of faith: if he loves, he is in the communion of love; if he prays, he is in the communion of prayer. Wherefore, no one can rest his hope in his own prayers; every one who prays asks the whole Church for intercession, not as if he had any doubts of the intercession of Christ, the one Advocate, but in the assurance that the whole Church ever prays for all her members. All the angels pray for us, the apostles, martyrs and patriarchs, and above them all the holy Mother of our Lord; and this holy unity is the true life of the Church. . . .

'Just as each of us requires prayers from all, so each person owes his prayers on behalf of all, the living and the dead, and even those who are yet unborn; for in praying as we do with all the Church, that the world may come to the knowledge of God, we pray not only for the present generation, but for those whom God will hereafter call into life. We pray for the living, that the grace of God may be upon them, and for the dead that they may become worthy of the vision of God's face. . . .

'But we pray in the Spirit of love, knowing that no one will be saved otherwise than by the prayer of the Church, in which Christ lives, knowing and trusting that, so long as the end of time has not come, all the members of the Church, both living and departed, are being perfected incessantly by mutual prayer. The saints whom God has glorified are much higher than we; but higher than all is the holy Church, which comprises within herself all the saints, and prays for all, as may be seen in the divinely inspired Liturgy. If, while worshipping and glorifying the saints, we pray that God may glorify them, we do not lay ourselves open to the charge of pride: for to us who have received permission to call God "Our Father", leave has also been granted to pray, "Hallowed be his Name, his Kingdom come, his will be done". And if we are permitted to pray to God that he will glorify his Name and accomplish his will, who will forbid us to pray him to glorify his saints, and to give repose to his elect? . . .

'Let no man say: "What prayer shall I apportion for the living and the departed, when my prayers are insufficient even for myself?" For if he is not able to pray, of what use would it be even to pray for himself? But in truth the Spirit of love prays in him. Likewise let him not say: "What is the good of my prayer for another, when he prays for himself, and Christ Himself intercedes for him?" But in truth the Spirit of love prays in him. Let him not say: "It is even now impossible to change the judgement of God"; for his prayer is included in the ways of God, and God foresaw it. If he be a member of the Church, his prayer is necessary for all her members. If the head should say that it did not require blood from the rest of the body, and that it would not give its own blood to it, the hand would wither. So a man is necessary to the Church as long as he is in her; and if he withdraws himself from communion with the Church, he perishes himself and will cease to be any longer a member of the Church. The Church prays for all, and we pray together for all; but our prayer must be true, and a true expression of love, and not a mere form of words. Not being able to love all men, we pray for those whom we love, and our prayer is not hypocritical: but we pray God that we may be able to love all, and pray for all without hypocrisy. Mutual prayer is the blood of the Church, and the glorification of God her breath. We pray in a spirit of love, not of interest; in the spirit of filial freedom, not of the law of the hireling demanding his pay. Every man who asks: "What use is there in prayer?" acknowledges himself to be in bondage. True prayer is true love.'

(ii) *The Universal Priesthood and the Ordained Ministry*

The conception of Authority in the patristic period included both the share of all Christians in the common worship and life of the believing and worshipping community, and the authority of the hierarchy, which began with the Apostles. The names of St. Cyprian and St. Augustine come to mind at once, as witnesses to this double truth. But in the middle ages the authority of the hierarchy received most of the emphasis, and the laity were relegated to a subordinate place.

Luther was the first to work out a theology of the Universal Priesthood of all Believers, bringing this phrase into prominence. As we shall see, his exposition is on the old lines; he criticizes heavily the Double Standard for the clerical class and the laity, for all alike share in the One Baptism, while at the same time he sees very clearly that the Sacred Ministry is of divine ordinance. So he keeps clearly in view what we today would call the 'polarity' of these two aspects. Luther, however, was no systematizer, as Calvin was. He sought to explain theological truths to the common people, and speak in their language; therefore he must take one point at a time. We shall also see how at certain points his exposition falls short; and one of these may be mentioned at once. Coming at the end of the Middle Ages, he had been accustomed to think of a priest as one who performed certain ritual actions in virtue of his individual possession of holy orders. So he tends to interpret the Universal Priesthood as meaning that each Christian is individually a priest; and here he is missing the point of the primary texts, Exodus 19.5–6 and 1 Peter 2.5 and 9, where the Royal Priesthood is for Israel as the holy nation, and for the Church as corporately the People of God. In Revelation 1.6 and 5.10, however, he had before him the 'Received Text',[1] in which the plural form is used, 'kings and priests'.

The positive truth which he proclaims with splendid power is that all baptized Christians have a priestly ministry in their

---

[1] The Hebrew text of Ex. 19.6 is best translated 'a kingdom-of-priests'; but it was not easy to put into Greek. The LXX renders it as *basileion hierateuma*, 'a royal priesthood'; and so it is in 1 Peter. The other Jewish translators however render it as 'a kingdom of priests', or as 'a kingdom and priests'. So we have according to the best manuscripts in Rev. 1.6 'a kingdom, priests', and in 5.10 'a kingdom and priests'; but the Received Text, which was printed from quite late manuscripts, reads 'kings and priests', and so it was in the text which Luther had, and in our A.V.

Ordained and Unordained Lay-men

several stations in life, whether as a prince or a farmer or an artisan or a merchant or in the ordinary sense a 'priest', and all alike are called to glorify God. In God's sight all are on one level; he is the Judge of all alike; all have the same responsibility before him. At the same time, the 'priest' is the dispenser not of earthly commodities but of heavenly things, God's word and sacraments, and so his station in life is of unique dignity and glory and of divine ordinance.

So Luther wrote in the *Address to the German Nobility* of 1520, that the notion that

'the pope and bishops and priests and monks belong to the "spiritual" order in society, and princes and squires and artisans and farmers to the "worldly" order, is all sheer falsehood, since all Christians belong in truth to the "spiritual" order' as St. Paul says in 1 Cor. 12 that we all are one body; there is one Baptism, one Gospel, one Faith. So in our baptism we were all ordained to be priests (1 Pet. 2.9 and Rev. 5.10). . . . Therefore ordination by a bishop means simply this—it is as if on behalf of the whole community, in which all have equal power, he took one from among them and appointed him to exercise this power on behalf of the others; as if ten brothers, of royal birth and holding equal rights to the inheritance, were to choose one of their number to manage the inheritance for them.'[1]

Here is a piece of Luther's popular exposition; it reminds us how in the early church the bishop was freely elected by the people. But questions arise. What would Luther have said if the choice of a local congregation in his day had fallen on a Zwinglian or an Anabaptist? There needs to be in the Church some sort of guardianship to control the appointment of Ministers. Another point is that Luther did think that any baptized person has power to administer the sacraments, on the ground that the supernatural and divine gift is given through the almighty divine word alone; hence any man might celebrate the sacrament as a priest for his own family, just as it could

---

[1] A free rendering, from Prenter, *Reformatoren Martin Luther*, pp. 47–8. The full text is in *Reformation Writings of Martin Luther* (Lee Wolff), I, 113–14.

Clergy and Lay-People

be his duty to speak to his neighbour some word of God. But in the New Testament the Eucharist is seen as the action of the assembled Church of God, even when its meeting is regularly held in some private house,[1] and there has always been the sense that each Eucharist, however few are present on a particular occasion, is still an action of the whole Church.[2] Luther's distinction, however, was that in the public service of the Church no man could administer the Sacrament or preach the Word, unless he had received authority from the Church to do so; only in private, in the home, might he do so.[3]

At the same time Luther believed and said most definitely that the Ministry is of divine institution. There, for instance, is his sermon of 1530, *On keeping children at school*, where he says of the sacred Ministry:

'I hope that the faithful and all who call themselves Christians know well that this spiritual office is instituted and founded by God, not with gold or silver but by the blood and the bitter death of his only Son our Lord Jesus Christ. For from his wounds proceed the sacraments, and he has in truth bought it for us at a price, that in the whole world there should be such a Ministry to preach, baptize, loose and bind sins, give the sacrament of the Lord's Supper, console and exhort with God's word, and whatever else belongs to the care of souls. . . . And it is solely because this Ministry has existed that human society is still in being, otherwise it would long since have perished.'[4]

And so in his *Von den Konsiliis und Kirchen* (1539), he says:

'There must be bishops or pastors or preachers, to administer publicly these four things (preaching, baptism, Eucharist, the keys), on behalf of and in the name of the Church, and much more, according to Christ's institution, as St. Paul says in Ephesians 4, "He gave gifts unto men," namely Apostles,

---

[1] ibid., p. 58; *Embedets guddomelige indstiftelse*, p. 90.
[2] p. 120 above.
[3] Bobrinskoy, p. 126 above.
[4] Luther, W. A., XXX, 2, pp. 526–30; quoted in *Reformatoren Martin Luther*, pp. 52–3.

Ordained and Unordained Lay-men

Prophets, Evangelists, Teachers, Pastors, etc. . . . . If Apostles, Evangelists and Prophets came to an end, others had to come in their place and continue to come, to the end of time.'[1]

Such is the 'polarity' of the Priesthood of All Believers on the one hand, and the divine ordinance of the Ordained Ministry on the other. Professor Prenter tries hard to show that Luther's thought in this matter was really self-consistent. But Luther was no systematic theologian, and though he knew and taught that both the Apostolic Ministry and the Universal Priesthood were there in the New Testament, it does not seem that he ever clearly worked out the relation between the two, nor made it clear to his successors. In the Lutheran churches today it is widely held and taught that the Ordained Ministry is a particular application of the Universal Priesthood, and Luther's teaching about the divine institution of the Ministry is forgotten or overlooked. As we shall see in a moment, such a view of the Ordained Ministry leads easily to a forgetfulness of the New Testament teaching that the Priesthood of All Christians depends directly on Christ's own Priesthood and the Church's life 'in Christ'—a point which Luther saw and taught very clearly.[2] With Luther, the Universal Priesthood was certainly not a 'democratic' conception.[3]

Dr. T. W. Manson, in the book already quoted in Chapter VI, says that 'in the *Apostolic Ministry* Bishop Kirk described the priesthood of all believers as "the decisive formula of all non-episcopal Christendom". Certainly it has been one of the rallying-cries of Free Churchmanship. But it may be suspected that some who use it most often and most emphatically mean by it something more like "the priesthood of no believer whatsoever", or "the non-priesthood of all believers". When the priesthood of all believers is construed in this way, it can readily become the ground for rejecting the idea, not only of a priestly order within the Church, but also of any ministerial order

[1] Luther, W. A., L, 632–4; *Embedets guddomelige indstiftelse*, p. 85.
[2] As in his 'On the Misuse of the Mass', W.A., VIII, 486; or his *De instituendis Ministris*, XI, 189, 411.
[3] Prenter, *Embedets guddomelige indstiftelse*, pp. 91–5.

whatsoever.'[1] His own study in that book was written to rescue the belief both in the universal priesthood and in the reality of the Ordained Ministry.

But the best statement of the relation of the two that I have heard is one that Bishop Lesslie Newbigin gave us in Australia in 1961:[2]

'The whole Church is a royal priesthood. The whole Church is to be the place where the love of God is made available for men, where the light of God shines upon men, so that they are no longer living in the fog of illusion but in the clear light of reality. . . . This priestly ministry of the whole Church is to be carried out through its entire membership. The Christian man at his daily task is the bearer of it. Is it not an illusion that constantly fogs our thinking about the Church that we think of it as something which exists manifestly on Sundays, is in a kind of state of suspended animation from Monday to Saturday, and unlike most animals, hibernates in summer? The truth is of course that the Church exists in its prime reality from Monday to Saturday, in all its members, dispersed through fields and homes and offices and factories, bearing the royal priesthood of Christ into every corner of the world. On the Lord's Day, it is withdrawn into itself to renew its being in the Lord himself, and supremely in that service which we call the Lord's Supper or Eucharist. . . .

'One of the tragic facts of Christian history has been the obscuring and distorting of this great scriptural doctrine of the royal priesthood of the whole Church, first by a clericalism which practically confined the priestly character to a professional ministry, and then by an understandable but lamentable counter-distortion which tried to assert the self-sufficient priesthood of every individual, apart from the organic unity of the priestly body of Christ.

[1] T. W. Manson, *Sacrifice and Priesthood, Christ's and Ours*, pp. 40–1.
[2] *We were Brought Together*, the Report of the National Conference of Australian Churches, held at Melbourne University, Feb. 2–11, 1960 (The Australian Council of Churches, 1960), pp. 96–7.

Ordained and Unordained Lay-men

'The truth is that it is only because this priestly body has been given a structure which includes a ministry based on and continuous with the ministry of the incarnate Lord himself, that there is a priestly character in the ministry answering to the priestly character of the body. And the supreme function of the ministry is so to minister that the whole body attains to and retains its true priestly character. What an unnecessary and pitiable thing it is to see these two things which belong together being placed against one another, so that a clericalism which denies the true priestly character of the *laos*, the consecrated people of God, produces a laicism which neglects the true service of the ordained ministry! And let me be bold to say, as one who comes from a wholly Protestant background, that modern Protestantism is as fertile as ancient Catholicism ever was in producing new and vigorous varieties of clericalism. . . . If you are an ordained minister of the Gospel, know that this is the highest possible definition of *your* ministry, that you should be servants of the servants of God, so ministering the things of Christ to your people and so equipping them for the work of ministry, as St. Paul says in another place, that everyone of them knows himself to be a part of the royal priesthood, the holy nation, and that every man is equipped for that priestly ministry.'

In our own day, Roman Catholic theologians are expounding with great power the place of the laity in relation to the clergy within the People of God, broadly along the same lines as those of Bishop Newbigin's exposition; we have seen something of this already in our summary of Père Congar's treatment of Authority in Chapter V, and he has developed the theme at length in his book *Lay-people in the Church*.[1] Practical expression is being given to this in noble evangelistic work such as that of the Mission de France, where the priests who are working in *équipes* (teams) in the de-christianized areas of the country are en-

[1] *Jalons de la théologie du laicat*, Paris. E.T., Burns and Oates (1957). Cf. J. M. Todd, 'The Authority of the Laity' in *Problems of Authority* (for which book see p. 71, note, above).

listing the active co-operation of the laity in more loosely-knit *équipes*, with regular meetings for discussion and prayer. I cannot refrain from citing a ceremonial expression of this which I saw in 1961 at the high mass in a church in Paris, where at the beginning of the Communion a pair of servers carrying candles proceeded down the main aisle into the nave, and returned shortly after to the sanctuary leading a procession of communicants. I thought that there could not be a finer ceremonial expression of the Priesthood of All Christians.

(iii) *Many Ministries*

One of the functions of the Ordained Ministry is *episkopē*, the pastoral care of souls. But others also share in *episkopē*. First there is the *episkopē* which belongs to the Family, which is the basic unit of human society; and here God has entrusted to fathers and mothers the care of their children and their up-bringing. This is a pastoral care of souls, which belongs in the first place to them. It is the primary justification of Infant Baptism that in a Christian family the children share in the life of a Christian household; and the question is raised in our day whether it is right that the baptism of children of non-Christian families should take place at all. For baptism is not a magical rite: it presupposes a Christian family life and up-bringing. All is in place where the parents exercise their duty of *episkopē*.

But this pastoral care of children is not limited to the home. There is also the school, and every schoolmaster and school-mistress shares in this pastoral duty, at all the levels of the educational system. Very many who are not Christians have a clear sense of this duty; and all Christian teachers see this as part of their responsibility before God.

And we cannot stop here. There are very many others who have a similar responsibility, by the fact that they have control over other people's lives: foremen in all the branches of industry, and all the higher grades up to the managers and directors, have responsibility for those whose lives they control. They fail

Ordained and Unordained Lay-men

in their duty if they look on those under their control as mere units of the machinery of industry, and forget that they are human persons. This respect for them as persons comes out often in cases of sickness, where one or another of those in control goes out of his way to give personal help. But it applies all the time; it is the thing that makes all the difference to a really well-run business concern, when it is seen and known that all those engaged in it are sharing in a co-operative activity. The same applies to all who bear responsibility in local government or national government. They too share in a kind of *episkopē*.

Then there are the social services: the work of the doctor and the nurse, in ministering not merely to 'cases' of sickness and disease, but to persons in sore need of help: that of governors of prisons and their staffs, of Probation Officers, and all who in various ways serve the unfortunate members of society who have fallen foul of the Law; and that of all who in various ways administer the services of the Welfare State. The principle which underlies all this is well stated by Bishop John Ramsbotham of Wakefield, in an essay on the ministry of the Suffragan Bishop:[1]

'The episcopal ministry, which includes the ministerial priesthood and diaconate, and has no meaning apart from our Lord's ministry and indeed is no more and no less than his ministry exercised through it, sums up and interprets all other kinds of personal responsibility for others which must exist in any ordered human society. From the Queen downwards through her prime minister and other ministers of state, through all in authority under her, through local government, through the social services, through the management of industrial and commercial organizations, right down to the humblest father and mother, the responsibility for other persons, looked at in the light of the episcopal ministry, may be seen to be a trust given by the Creator and Ruler of all souls, to whom the holder of the trust is ultim-

[1] In *Bishops*, a volume of essays edited by the Rt. Rev. Glyn Simon, Bishop of Llandaff. The Faith Press, London (1961), pp. 95–6

ately answerable. And the people who have to be looked after, or managed, or governed, or taught, or nursed, whatever it may be, are not just figures with a number, but individual souls for whom Christ died.'

It is plain that in all this women have their full share. This is especially clear in our own day, when women receive the same education as men, and take university degrees, and become professors and head-mistresses of schools, and teachers in schools; and some of them become theologians and some become wise directors of souls. Such was the late Evelyn Underhill, who used to conduct retreats for clergy. Yet this is not wholly a new thing: there have been saintly figures such as St. Catherine of Siena, Mother Julian of Norwich, and above all St. Teresa of Avila, one of the wisest of all the masters of the spiritual life. From the early days of the Religious life onwards there have been the women's Religious Communities, in which Mother Superiors and other gifted Sisters have exercised *episkopē* in the pastoral care of souls, writing books, preaching and teaching, and giving expert guidance in the individual ministry to souls which is of more real importance than that which is given in public discourses.

It is not for me, at this late stage in this book, to go into the question whether women ought to be ordained to the priesthood. The point that must be emphatically made here is that at present the Church is not giving to women the opportunity to serve in the Church as they ought, and that more and more in the future it must take action about this. God has made human beings male and female: the male and female are different, and have different capacities. All is wrong when the woman becomes ashamed of her femininity and behaves like a man. It is very clear that women can render distinguished services as Ministers of the Word, both in scholarship and in teaching and preaching, and in personal ministry to souls. Such capacities must be recognized and used far more than they are. Perhaps the answer will come increasingly as our church habits become more fluid and less formalized; the distinction will be drawn between formal liturgical worship and many kinds of less formal gatherings for teaching and discussion, in which the Minister of the Word of God will not be expected to come into church vested in a surplice with a robed choir.

(iv) *The Will of God in Social Life*

One more point must be raised before we end this chapter. It is all very well to talk of the Universal Priesthood and of the ministry of the servants of God in fields and homes and offices and factories. But what do they do when they are there? What does it involve and what does it cost, to be servants of God in this distressed and distracted modern world? It will not do for those who have been brought up in a respectable upper-middle-class tradition to go out into the world of industry and think that they are doing the will of God if they simply reflect the pattern of thought for which the Conservative Party has stood in the past. There is a whole wide world with its ways of thought and problems and needs, in which the Christian is sent to bear witness to Christ the Saviour of mankind.

But here we need again the help of Lesslie Newbigin, in the set of discourses from which I have quoted already.[1] He puts the problem in an Indian setting: but it is not specially an Indian problem, but one that faces Christians in England and in every land.

'To frame the question, "Should a Christian be involved in politics?" is to frame a question upon a falsehood. The only proper way to frame the question is to ask, "Is the Christian willing to bring his political decisions under the rule of Christ, or not? Is he going to allow his faith to control all his decisions, or only a limited section of his decisions, namely those which concern his personal and family ethics?"'

'Not long ago I was invited to spend an evening in India with a layman's group. It consisted of lawyers and doctors and teachers, many of them in Government service. Looking at the composition of the group, and the title "Christian Laymen's Group", I took three issues for my talk which

[1] *We were Brought Together*, pp. 101–2.

seemed to me to raise live questions for the Christian conscience of these men. I took the question of the debate which
was going on at the time, and in which lawyers were deeply
involved, regarding alterations to the Fundamental-rights
clauses of the Constitution. I took the question of the high-
pressure campaign being conducted by the Madras Government to secure the sterilization of married men having more
than three children. And I took the drive of the Education
Department in favour of common syncretistic worship in
schools as a means of achieving national unity.

'Each of these issues would have involved a deep-going and
painful discussion. It would perhaps have involved painful
and costly decisions on the part of those present. There are,
to use the apostolic language, "human institutions"[1] involved on both sides: the State, with its concern for social
order and well-being, with its duty to look ahead for the
future of the nation: the School, with its concern for develop-
ing responsible community life in which all communities can
participate: the Family, with its requirement that the integrity of the relations of husband and wife, parents and
children, be safeguarded. And finally, there was the need
to safeguard the integrity of the human person. But I found
that the group was entirely unwilling to have these questions
raised. At the end of my address discussion was abruptly fore-
closed with a call to prayer by the chairman. (*Laughter*) They
would have welcomed and followed up a talk on personal
evangelism, on prayer, on the fruit of the Spirit. They were
not prepared, as Christians, to face their actual moral
choices as professional men. That part, the major part, of
their waking life was to be kept out of the realm of faith,
outside of the rule of Christ.

'I am sure that any exposition of this passage which leads
to that kind of conclusion is wrong. "Be subject to every
human institution" cannot mean "Evade all responsibility

[1] 'Be subject, for the Lord's sake, to every human institution (*or* every
institution ordained for man)', I Peter 2.13. This was the text of his
discourse.

as Christians for the decisions you make as citizens, as employers, as trade unionists, or professional men." '

That these questions were put to Indians is quite accidental. Similar questions could be put in any country, such as, to quote Lesslie Newbigin again (p. 110), these two, of which the second is harder than the first:

(a) 'A man in a big store is expected to persuade customers to buy a product which he knows to be worthless. Does he obey the orders of his employer, or does he challenge the firm and risk starvation for himself and his dependants?'

(b) 'On a second level, a professional man becomes aware that the standard of professional ethics in his profession is basically wrong. How far ought he to go in defying the professional standard and risking the loss of status and livelihood for himself and his dependants?'

The individual Christian cannot carry the burden of answering such questions all by himself. He needs the help of others who are involved in them with him; for the questions come at him out of the social order to which we all belong. These more difficult questions are the object of what we call today 'Frontier Studies', of the frontier between the Gospel and the world which runs across every place where men live and work. The answers which are to be found are not only the answers of a few experts within the Church, but also of the Church itself in the persons of its members dispersed through the world, functioning through regular meetings for serious discussion.

There are many simpler questions, where it is not so hard for Christians-in-council to see the right way. And all the answers depend on a right view of the nature of man and on a Christian conception of 'the integrity of the human person'. The white man in South Africa gives an answer to the problem of *Apartheid* by courtesy, or discourtesy, to the black man in the store; and likewise the white man who meets a black man in London. The Christian layman will give the right answer if he truly believes in his heart that he is a layman, a member of the *Laos*, the People of God, to which every human being is called to belong, because Christ died for all and to all the Holy Spirit is given.

CHAPTER IX

Non-Episcopal and Episcopal Ministries

★

(i) *Non-Episcopal Ministries*

Gregory Dix wrote in *The Apostolic Ministry*, pp. 295–6:
'We should all be a long step nearer agreement if we recognized that the modern Protestant Societies cannot be "given" or "asked to accept" *episkopē* in the ancient sense[1] at all, because they already have it. It is an inseparable accompaniment of any corporate Christian life, and the Protestant ministries have every right to be suspicious of our attempts to thrust a merely "Administrative" episcopate upon them, as casting doubts upon the reality of their ministerial office. All the Reformed ministries of the sixteenth century reproduced, at least in intention and function, the primitive *zeqenim* (Elders or Presbyters) of the local Churches, as these would have been had there never been any "apostolate". The Calvinists may have reproduced the actual arrangements of the Judaeo-Christian presbyteries with less inexactness than the Lutherans and Independents, though even they achieved little of the antiquarian correctness which they sought, owing to the historical ignorance which the sixteenth century inherited from the mediaeval Latin Church. But all the Reformed ministries alike were by intention what the *zeqenim* had been, public ministries to God with an ecclesiastical authority from a particular society of Christians. As such

[1] For the meaning of *episkopē*, see p. 51 above.

143

they have a real pastoral office and authority, and a responsibility in and for the Society which has chosen and authorized them to guide its Christian life, to teach, to baptize, to celebrate the Lord's Supper, and even—like the Jewish "presbyteries"—to "hand on the Spirit" by the laying on of hands on others to fill up their own number. All this is *episkopē*. And inasmuch as these ministries are the freely chosen organs of their own Societies to exercise it, they are in one respect better entitled to the style of *episkopoi* in the ancient sense than the Anglican nominees of the State. We Anglicans complacently forget that election by his own Church was as much a requirement *sine qua non* for the "episcopate" of a pre-Nicene bishop as his consecration by the hands of other bishops.'

Two comments may be made on this. In the second sentence, the words 'our attempts to thrust a merely administrative episcopate upon them' may perhaps have been intended by Dom Gregory to refer to the scheme for the South Indian Church which was inaugurated nine months after *The Apostolic Ministry* was published; but I do not know whether this was in his mind when he wrote this passage. If it was, the history of the South Indian Church has abundantly disproved it. But those words are directly illustrated by Archbishop Fisher's suggestion made in his famous Cambridge Sermon, which was preached just a month before our book was published, that the non-episcopal Churches might well 'take episcopacy into their systems'. It has been pointed out[1] that if that suggestion had been acted upon, the result could have been that in one street there might be an Anglican church-building and a Presbyterian-Episcopal one and a Methodist-Episcopal one, belonging to congregations which, with occasional acts of Intercommunion, still continued to live their separate denominational lives.

A second comment must be that I cut short my quotation at the point where I did, because the next sentence contains a statement which I am sure is unsound and cannot stand up to

[1] By John Robinson, Bishop of Woolwich, in *On being the Church in the World*, S.C.M. (1960), pp. 101–3.

criticism; it is that 'all the evidence that we possess suggests that the *zeqenim* (the Christian presbyters) received their ordination not from their fellows but from the *shaliach*', i.e. the apostle. All the direct evidence that we possess consists of Acts 14.24, where Paul and Barnabas appoint 'Elders in every city' in the newly evangelized places, and 2 Timothy 1.6, where Timothy is reminded of his ordination by St. Paul. But there is other evidence. When Paul founded Churches, he did not stay there too long, lest by exercising direct control over everything that was done there he should spoil his newly planted Church by not allowing them freedom to grow. That this was a matter of deliberate policy has been demonstrated by Roland Allen in his important book *Missionary Methods: St. Paul's or Ours?*[1] He left them, having imparted to them all that was needed for a sound and healthy church life—namely, the 'tradition' of the Gospel itself (1 Cor. 15.1–3), of the Sacraments (1 Cor. 11.23), and of a Ministry of presbyters having power (in Dom Gregory's words) 'to "hand on the Spirit" by the laying on of hands on others to fill up their own number', which as he notices was the practice of the Jewish presbyteries. That it was the practice of the Christian presbyteries also is strongly suggested, as we have seen on p. 63, by the wording of Hippolytus's ordination rite for presbyters and by the fact that the existing presbyters continued to lay their hands on the new presbyters. Further, there is no evidence that every ordination of presbyters in the apostolic age had to be held up till an apostle could be found to preside; just as it is most improper to infer from Acts 8.17 and 19.6 that every baptism had to wait for an apostle to give Confirmation. It would seem then that we must assume that the apostles gave authority to the presbyters in the Churches to act as the Jewish presbyteries did.

[1] Roland Allen, *Missionary Methods: St. Paul's or Ours.* Published in 1912, revised 1927, and republished in 1960 by the World Dominion Press. I have given an account of his work in Chapter III of my book, *God's Kingdom and Ours.* S.C.M. Press (1959).

Non-Episcopal and Episcopal

(ii) *A Roman Catholic View*

Fr. E. H. Schillebeeckx, O.P., who is Professor at the Catholic Institute at Nymegen, and a greatly honoured name in Holland, gives in a book which has been translated into French with the title *Le Christ, Sacrement de la Rencontre de Dieu*,[1] a study on pp. 221–35 of 'The Religious Value of Sacraments in the Separated Christian Churches', with special reference of course to the Reformed Church of the Netherlands.

He begins by expounding the difference between Catholic and Protestant terminology, which is such that the two sides speak different theological languages. The result is that in the end he acknowledges that the things which the Protestants affirm, in their own theological language, are true. The Catholic starts with a conception of the Divine Order in creation and redemption, and expresses this in a systematic form and in scholastic language; hence he is bound to say that Protestant sacraments and ministries are 'invalid'. To the Protestant, however, 'valid' means the same as 'efficacious'; for he starts with the proclamation of the Word of God, of the Gospel of God, and he thinks throughout of the Gospel proclaimed and accepted by the personal response of faith, which is the work of the Holy Spirit in the believing community (pp. 222–7).

Then Dr. Schillebeeckx quotes the question put to some Catholics in Germany by the Lutheran Hans Asmussen: 'Do you desire that we should cease to celebrate our Lord's Supper since we are heretical, or do you rejoice in our sacramental life?' (p. 227), and proceeds to give his own answer to it. He begins with a sympathetic description of the Rite as it is celebrated by the Dutch Reformed Church, which, he says, is clearly a community which expresses in its worship its faith in Christ (pp. 229–31). After this, he goes on to examine the position, following strictly the teaching of St. Thomas Aquinas.

[1] Les Editions du Cerf, 'Lex Orandi' series, No. 21. Paris (1960). The title of the original, in the 3rd edition (1959), is, *Christus sacrament van de godsontmoeting*. 't Groeit, Antwerp, and H. Nelissen, Bilthoven.

A Roman Catholic View

St. Thomas teaches that even pagan rites, and still more Jewish rites, have a certain relation to Christ the Fulfiller; much more, then, will Protestant rites have some sort of sacramental validity, since the intention is to do what Christ commanded; even though their rite is not the Catholic sacrament, and is in some ways liturgically defective.

In St. Thomas we find certain further principles. Baptism points forward to the Eucharist (*Summa*, III, 65.3; 73.3); all baptism is baptism into the Church, and these Protestants are baptized. Then, just as there can be a 'baptism of desire' (on the part of persons who had desired baptism, but had been prevented by the act of persecutors from being baptized with water), and this is real baptism, so there can be a 'Eucharist of desire'; and this is more than the 'spiritual communion' of which St. Augustine speaks,[1] for it is a 'spiritual reception', mediated in some rite, of the Catholic sacrament itself. So then these baptized Protestants have in their Holy Supper something more than 'spiritual communion', for they are obeying Christ's own command; and they 'spiritually' receive the Catholic sacrament itself (pp. 232–3). This would not hold good if they were formally rejecting or refusing the Catholic sacrament; but they are not doing so. So,

'though the Evangelical Lord's Supper is not a valid sacrament, even partially, it is a quasi-sacramental expression of an explicit eucharistic desire, which implicitly seeks the actual benefits which the Catholic sacrament conveys. This gives it an objective religious validity, with a real relation to the Catholic Eucharist . . .' (p. 234).

He concludes:

'Even though it is our apostolic duty to desire the return of Protestants to the true Eucharist, we are bound to rejoice when we see them leading in good faith an intense and frequent sacramental life, and through their celebration of the Supper truly growing in union with Christ and with their fellow-men. Paradoxical as it may seem, this celebration is a

---

[1] This is familiar to us Anglicans from the rubric in our own form for the Communion of the Sick.

genuine act of prayer *ut omnes unum sint*. And when the
World Council of Churches meets together with the desire
to reach through theological conversations a fuller unity of
the Church, a Lord's Supper celebrated then by all together
will be a greater contribution to ecumenical unity than the
theological dialogue which is none the less necessary' (pp.
234–5).

We wonder and rejoice at such an argument as this, couched
in the strictest terms of the official theology, yet showing so
generous a good will and reaching so positive a conclusion. We
Anglicans may well reflect on this, recollecting that according
to the official Roman Catholic view our own sacraments and
orders are invalid.

These testimonies of Dix and Schillebeeckx have not been
quoted lightly. But since we Anglicans sometimes appear to
others to be guilty of 'double-think'—of giving with one hand
and taking it back with the other—on this very question, it is
important that a statement should be made here.

Churches lacking Episcopacy which have a right faith in
Jesus Christ and bring forth the fruit of the Spirit must be
reckoned to be within the Church of God and not outside it,
because Baptism is baptism into the one Body of Christ which
is his Church, and is his holy Temple, his Bride, his Flock.
Extra ecclesiam nulla salus means that all who are saved belong
to Christ's Church.

If such churches[1] are in error in lacking Episcopacy, that
does not mean that they are not within the Church; for the
visible Church on earth is composed of men who are subject to
temptation and sin, and so, as our Article XIX says, churches
in various places, including that of Rome, 'have erred' both in
their life and their liturgical practice and in matters of faith.[2]
We have seen in this book how the mediaeval church fell into

---

[1] It is of course an improper use of words to call denominations 'churches';
for in the New Testament the word *ecclesia* means 'the Church of God', and
'a church', such as that of Ephesus, is a local unit of the Church.

[2] The words are: 'As the Church of *Jerusalem, Antioch* and *Alexandria* have
erred; so also the Church of *Rome* hath erred, not only in their living and
manner of Ceremonies, but also in matters of Faith.'

grave error in these ways; and if in spite of those errors it retained its character as part of the Church of God, it becomes difficult to argue that those who honestly and in good faith laboured to reform those errors thereby put themselves outside the Church of God. Therefore the churches which sprang out of the Reformation are to be reckoned as part of the Church, and their ministries to be real ministries, in spite of the fact that a variety of errors which need to be remedied are found within those churches. The remedying of those faults and errors can, however, never be brought about by hostile criticism from without, but always and in each case by the healing action of the Holy Spirit from within.

(iii) *Ways to Unity*

We must turn next to consider the possibilities of actual Church Unity. It is important for us in Britain to realize how self-evidently urgent is the need for it in Africa and Asia, and that it only appears less urgent for us in Europe because we have for centuries past become fossilized in our divisions. But Christians can become one only where there is real concord and agreement, of the sort that comes slowly, as divided Christians come to know one another and to respect one another. Christian Unity is on the way; but we have got to be patient and be prepared to be led by the truth which the Holy Spirit teaches, and to bear always in mind that the Holy Spirit is given also to those from whom we differ.

Christian Unity is on the way. It is agreed on all sides that the Episcopal Ministry is the necessary framework of reunited Christendom; and it is coming to be understood more and more widely that Episcopacy is not a mere form of church government, and that it may not be identified with mediaeval prelacy or with modern administrative bureaucracy, but that it is a sacred office, a *mysterion*, as the Lambeth Conference of 1930 explained to the visiting Eastern Orthodox. As we have emphasized in this book, it is not merely that it goes back to the second century when bishops appeared in the Church in succession to the apostles, but that it is in itself a witness to the Gospel.

Here, then, is one theological fact. Another theological fact is that the non-episcopal ministries must be reckoned to be real ministries of the Word and Sacraments, having regularly constituted authority within organized societies of Christians; and that if it is acknowledged that they are Christian societies, then they are part of the Church, which is the body of Christ and 'the blessed company of all faithful people'. Since then these non-episcopal societies arose out of the Reformation, it was necessary in this book to make a study of the Reformation, on the background of the failures of the mediaeval church in regard to the nature of Christian Authority and the right relation of clergy and laity; this failure was reflected also in mediaeval liturgical practice. But while we acknowledge that the Reformation was a return to the Gospel, and a proclamation of certain right principles, we must acknowledge also that in the churches based on the Reformation, including the Church of England, those principles have not found fully adequate expression in liturgy and teaching and life. Nevertheless there has been splendid witness borne to the Christian faith in these churches, and the fruit of the Spirit has been manifest.

Here then are two theological facts; and the problem of Unity between episcopal and non-episcopal churches is the problem of correlating them in practice. In regard to this, two Ways of Unity have emerged, which we must now consider; but it must be borne in mind as we do so that these two Ways deal with only one part of the whole problem of Unity. When we think of the *whole* estate of Christ's Church, it is apparent that the major problem is that of the ancient churches of the West and of the East, the Roman Catholic Church and the Orthodox Churches, first in their relations with one another, and then in their relations with us who at the Reformation became separated from the main body of the Western Church.

Of these two Ways of Unity, the first is what is most conveniently called the *South Indian Way*, on the basis of which the present Church of South India was formed in 1947; and it is this. After conversations and negotiations involving full discussion of all points of principle, a Union is inaugurated, on the basis of unity in the Faith, and with a constitutional Episcopacy as the given symbol and efficacious sign of unity; all the Ordained Ministers of the Uniting Churches are accepted as Presbyters of the United Church; and all ordinations after Union are to be episcopal. It is also still possible for Ministers from what used to be called the 'sending Churches' to come into the South Indian Church, during the period when the Churches in Europe and elsewhere are still in a divided condition. The English Convocations, which in 1950, three years after the Union, were not able to come to an agreed decision about the South Indian Church, decided in 1955 that ordinations by its Bishops were to be accepted as valid.

In such a United Church there is bound to be for thirty or more years after the Union a diminishing number of Presbyters who have not been episcopally ordained, while the number of those episcopally ordained increases every year. It would seem that where the episcopal office is as highly valued and honoured as it is in South India, the Presbyters not episcopally ordained would be bound to feel, at least in their hearts, a certain sense that they have missed something valuable; though it does not appear that any such feeling finds expression within the South Indian Church. But in the Interim Report of the Anglican-Methodist Conversations issued in 1958,[1] we learn that this 'South Indian Way', which had been proposed in England in 1937 in the document entitled *Church Relations in England*, was turned down because for thirty or more years general Intercommunion with the Church of England would not be possible, and what we shall call in a moment 'the Lanka Way' was recommended.

The principle of the 'South Indian Way' is accepted by the Taizé Community of the French Reformed Church, in so far as Brothers from all the evangelical Churches are accepted as

---

[1] *Conversations between the Church of England and the Methodist Church: An Interim Statement.* S.P.C.K. and Epworth Press (1958), Ch. VI.

eligible to join the Community, and those who have been ordained in any of the Churches are accepted as Pastors, for celebrating the sacraments and giving absolution. It seems quite safe to say that this Way will similarly be accepted by all Religious Communities which may be formed within the non-episcopal Churches in the future, and that all such Communities or Houses of Prayer will have a rule of Intercommunion for all their members, and probably for all visitors who come to stay with them for more than a day or two, because the Eucharist will necessarily be the central act of their worship.

The second way may be called for convenience the *Way of Lanka*, which is common to the schemes for Church Union in Ceylon (Lanka) and in North India and Pakistan. This is a variant of the 'South Indian Way', and it proposes the unification from the start not only of the Episcopal Ministry but of the Presbyteral also. This Way was described in the first pages of this book, pp. 13–14. The key-points are, first, that all the Ordained Ministries of the Uniting Churches are recognized to be real Ministries of the Word and Sacraments, and second, that after the constitution of the Episcopal Ministry in the United Church, the Bishop of each diocese is to lay hands on all the Ordained Ministers to make them Presbyters of the Church of God within this particular United Church.

The result of the debates in the English Convocations was, as we have seen, that the plans for church union in Ceylon and in North India and Pakistan failed to receive assent, and were virtually rejected. If I may dare to interpret the minds of those who spoke against the proposals—on the basis of a longish correspondence with an old friend who was one of them—it would seem that the difficulties were these: first, an uncertainty whether the non-episcopal Ministries ought to be reckoned as Real Ministries in the Church of God, as being 'invalid'; second, an objection to the proposed Rite of Unification of the presbyteral ministries, since it would carry different meanings to those from episcopal and those from non-episcopal churches who took part in it, and it appeared to be left uncertain whether it would involve a valid Ordination of the men who

had not been episcopally ordained; and third, I think, a sus-
picion that there would be a lurking confusion in the minds of
some between Ordination proper and a 'wider commission'—
namely, to put it concretely, a commission to an Anglican (for
instance) to minister to Methodists and others to whom he had
previously not been authorized to minister. This last point links
up with various notions which had been current for some time
previously about 'degrees of validity' in various ministries, and
an uncertainty whether these notions lay behind the proposed
plans for Union.

How far, then, did the objection lie to the plan itself as set
out for instance in the printed Scheme proposed for Ceylon?
and how far was it based on a lack of clarity about the theological issues? In other words, if those who were to take part in the
Schemes were theologically clear, and knew exactly what was
to be done in the proposed Rite, could the Rite itself be
accepted as satisfactory? The leaders in Ceylon and in North
India and Pakistan believed this;[1] I have attempted to express
what they said in the last sentence of the paragraph at the top
of p. 14 above. They recognized that the uniting Churches
represented different traditions, and they looked on the Rite
as a prayer to the Lord of the Church for a new creative act to
initiate a healing of a schism within the Church which is his
Body.

The theological uncertainty however remains; and it has
been a main object of this book to do something at least to clear
it up. For if Christians are to come together into Unity, they
must agree about what they are doing; otherwise the unity
achieved will not be real unity. But Christian Unity is on the
way, and the questions raised by the South Indian Way and
the Lanka Way must continue to be discussed, till there is
agreement about the answer. We may take encouragement
from the fact that the English Convocations, which had not

---

[1] See the *Scheme* and the *Plan* for Ceylon and North India/Pakistan
respectively, which are conveniently reprinted in *Ceylon, North India and
Pakistan* by Bishop Bayne. S.P.C.K. (1960). Also an article by Canon Sully
in the *Church Quarterly Review*, April–June 1961, on 'Uniting the Ministries'.

been prepared to reach any decision about the South Indian Church in 1950, gave an affirmative answer in 1955.

The problem of the union of episcopal and non-episcopal Churches is only a part of the whole problem of Christian Unity, for it concerns only the churches which have sprung out of the Reformation in the West. There is also the wider problem of the unity between the West and the East, between the Roman Catholic Church and the Eastern Orthodox Churches. In this book I have included no discussion of the Papacy and the claim of the Roman Bishop to be the only possible Primate of all Christendom. Yet year by year the preliminary work goes on; year by year there is an increase of mutual approaches and contacts, including those non-controversial contacts which take place on the level of the spiritual life, which are possibly the most important of all. And this year, 1962, the Second Vatican Council is to meet. The time for direct approaches to Unity has not yet come; but it will come.

Another problem of Unity, which also this book has not dealt with at all, is that which is presented by the 'Fundamentalist' wing of Christendom, which refuses so far to take much part in the ecumenical movement. It comprises the 'conservative evangelicals' within the Anglican communion, and similar groups among Presbyterians, Methodists and others, with the Inter-Varsity Fellowship of Evangelical Unions (I.V.F.), the Faith Missions, and among the sects the Pentecostalists who are basically orthodox in belief. All these are characterized by intense zeal and a wonderful self-sacrificing devotion which they draw out from all their members; but they have little sense of what the rest of Christendom means by 'the Church', and they hold apart from the World Council of Churches, regarding it as wrongly tolerant of heresy and misbelief, as it does not hold to the infallibility of the Word of God in Holy Scripture. Yet some of the Pentecostalists were admitted to the World Council of Churches at New Delhi in 1961. Besides the orthodox sects, there are the Jehovah's Witnesses and others who are by all standards heretical, but share the zeal and self-devotion of the other sects. Nothing has been said in this book about this wing of Christendom, because we have been occupied with traditional Christianity; but it also is part of the problem of Unity.

Yet Unity is on the way, and a New Reformation is on the way, both of the Protestant Reformation and of the Counter-Reformation; and it is bringing a day of new hope for us all. It is for faith to discern in the things which are happening, and will by God's gracious mercy continue to happen, a new creative action by the Lord of the Church, for the binding up of that which has been broken and a healing of that which is diseased, in the Church which is his Body. This new-creative action will be a raising up of the Church by the Holy Spirit to newness of life in the carrying on of its mission to the non-Christian countries and to de-christianized Europe. In the days to come the Episcopal Ministry, in which the non-episcopal Churches will have come to share, will be the given centre of Christian Unity in each locality. The episcopal office will take new forms, while continuing to be what it is. Already in England it seems incongruous that a Bishop should rank as a Peer of the Realm, and be designated as the 'Lord Bishop'; for his proper authority is a spiritual authority, as servant of the Lord Jesus Christ and therefore 'servant of the servants of God'. There is much to break down, much to build, much to restore.

I will add as a sort of epilogue the statement of the Office and Function of the Bishop, which was promised in the first chapter.

(iv) *The Office of the Bishop*

The Apostles of Jesus continued, after his death and resurrection and in the power of the Holy Spirit, the proclamation of his Gospel-message of the Kingdom and Reign of God, and exercised pastoral care of the Church-community composed of those who had been born again into the new life; and the Bishops are their successors in this proclamation and this ministry.

The Office of the Bishop then symbolizes and expresses—
(a) as regards *episkopē* or pastoral care:

—the guardianship of the preaching of the Word, including right doctrine and the exclusion of false teachings;

—the ministry of the sacraments, since he is the primary liturgical minister of his diocese; he ordains the priests to whom the direct charge of the Flock is delegated, while it remains his as well as theirs, and he confirms each one who by Baptism has been admitted into the Church;

—the administration of his diocese, with the help of archdeacons and others, and the exercise of discipline over clergy and people; but always not as a ruler or a judge, but as a Father-in-God.

(b) as regards Unity:

—he is (ideally and properly) the centre of unity of all the Christians in his diocese; thus in a multi-racial community he is and is seen to be the Father-in-God of people of all races:

—his Office symbolizes the unity of all Christians *in time*, since the succession expresses the oneness of the Church of today with that of all past generations and of those yet to come.

—and the unity of all Christians *in place*, since he meets with other Bishops in General Synods and Councils, where he represents his own diocese to them, and them to it. This is illustrated by the fact that he is consecrated by at least three Bishops from outside his diocese, some of whom may be Bishops of other races from overseas.

(c) His responsibility is a personal responsibility. He is to take counsel, as for instance with his Synod; but he is not subject, as the head officers of some other Churches are today, to majority votes for which no individual voter is responsible, and so must himself carry the responsibility for decisions, for which he is responsible to the Lord. He may not therefore rule as an autocrat, for he is set to rule in the Church and with the Church rather than over it.

Index

Index